Noom Diet M

Transform Your Life with This Ultimate Guide and Cookbook, Featuring 120 Irresistible Noom Diet Meal Prep Recipes to Save Time and Stay on Track

<u>Skylar Nourish</u>

Visit our channel

https://www.youtube.com/channel/UCRIcfFfoZQveWSafy7bf4ng

NUTRIBITES
SKYLAR NOURISH

Subscribe to our YouTube Channel

THIS CERTIFICATE IS AWARDED TO

Skylar Nourish

© Copyright 2023 by NutriBites - All rights reserved.

The following Book is reproduced below with the goal of providing information that is as accurate and reliable as possible. Regardless, purchasing this Book can be seen as consent to the fact that both the publisher and the author of this book are in no way experts on the topics discussed within and that any recommendations or suggestions that are made herein are for entertainment purposes only. Professionals should be consulted as needed prior to undertaking any of the action endorsed herein.

This declaration is deemed fair and valid by both the American Bar Association and the Committee of Publishers Association and is legally binding throughout the United States. Furthermore, the transmission, duplication, or reproduction of any of the following work including specific information will be considered an illegal act irrespective of if it is done electronically or in print. This extends to creating a secondary or tertiary copy of the work or a recorded copy and is only allowed with the express written consent from the Publisher. All additional right reserved.

The information in the following pages is broadly considered a truthful and accurate account of facts and as such, any inattention, use, or misuse of the information in question by the reader will render any resulting actions solely under their purview. There are no scenarios in which the publisher or the original author of this work can be in any fashion deemed liable for any hardship or damages that may befall them after undertaking information described herein.

Additionally, the information in the following pages is intended only for informational purposes and should thus be thought of as universal. As befitting its nature, it is presented without assurance regarding its prolonged validity or interim quality. Trademarks that are mentioned are done without written consent and can in no way be considered an endorsement from the trademark holder.

TABLE OF CONTENT

    1.1 The Noom Diet Explained 10
    1.2 The Importance of Meal Prep in Your Noom Diet Journey 10
    1.3 Setting Up Your Kitchen for Success 11

Chapter 2: Stocking Your Pantry for Noom Diet Meal Prep 12

    2.1 Essential Noom Diet Ingredients 12
    2.2 Creating a Noom-Friendly Shopping List 12
    2.3 Organizing Your Pantry for Noom Meal Prep 13

Chapter 3: Green Foods: The Foundation of the Noom Diet 14

    3.1 Understanding Green Foods 14
    3.2 Top Green Foods for Meal Prep 14
    3.3 Green Foods Recipes for a Busy Week 15

Chapter 4: Yellow Foods: Moderation is Key 17

    4.1 The Role of Yellow Foods in the Noom Diet 17
    4.2 Incorporating Yellow Foods in Your Meal Prep 17
    4.3 Delicious Yellow Food Recipes 18

Chapter 5: Red Foods: Indulging Mindfully 19

    5.1 Understanding Red Foods 19
    5.2 Tips for Including Red Foods in Your Meal Prep 19
    5.3 Guilt-Free Red Food Recipes 20

Chapter 6: Meal Prep Strategies for Long Work Weeks and Busy Days 22

    6.1 Embracing Batch Cooking and Freezing 22
    6.2 Incorporating Slow Cooker and Instant Pot Meals 22
    6.3 Creating a Meal Prep Schedule 23
    6.4 Time-Saving Meal Prep Tips 23

Chapter 7: Customizing Your Meal Prep for Dietary Preferences and Allergies 24

7.1 Adapting Noom Recipes for Vegetarians and Vegans 24

7.2 Adjusting Recipes for Gluten-Free Diets 25

7.3 Managing Food Allergies and Sensitivities 26

7.4 Creating a Balanced and Personalized Meal Plan 26

Chapter 8: Staying Motivated and Overcoming Meal Prep Obstacles 27

8.1 Identifying Common Meal Prep Challenges 27

8.2 Keeping Your Meal Prep Fresh and Exciting 27

8.3 Time Management Strategies for Meal Prep 29

8.4 Building Culinary Confidence 29

Chapter 9: Meal Prep for Weight Loss Plateaus and Maintaining Progress 30

9.1 Navigating Weight Loss Plateaus 30

9.2 Strategies for Overcoming Plateaus with Meal Prep 30

9.3 Maintaining Your Progress with Meal Prep 32

Chapter 10: Incorporating Exercise and Mindfulness into Your Noom Diet Journey 33

10.1 The Importance of Exercise 33

10.2 Finding the Right Exercise Routine 33

10.3 Mindfulness and the Noom Diet 34

Chapter 11: Making the Noom Diet a Sustainable Lifestyle Choice 35

11.1 The Importance of Sustainability 35

11.2 Long-Term Meal Prep Strategies 35

11.4 Staying Accountable and Supported 37

11.5 Embracing a Holistic Approach to Wellness 37

Chapter 12: Celebrating Your Success and Planning for the Future 38

12.1 Acknowledging Your Achievements 38

12.2 Setting New Health and Wellness Goals 38

12.4 Lifelong Learning and Growth 40

12.5 Inspiring Others with Your Success 40

BREAKFAST RECIPES 41

Green Smoothie Bowl 41

Overnight Chia Pudding with Berries 42

Veggie Egg White Scramble 43

Greek Yogurt Parfait with Fresh Fruit and Granola 43
Protein-Packed Quinoa Porridge 44
Banana Oat Pancakes 44
Smoked Salmon and Avocado Toast 45
Spinach and Feta Egg Muffins 46
Almond Butter and Apple Rice Cake 46
Mixed Berry Protein Smoothie 47
Cauliflower Hash Browns with Salsa 48
Whole Wheat Breakfast Burrito with Black Beans 49
Zucchini and Tomato Frittata 50
Peanut Butter and Banana Smoothie 51
Sweet Potato and Kale Breakfast Hash 52
Blueberry Protein Muffins 53
Avocado and Egg Toast 54
Oatmeal Breakfast Cookies 55
Chia Seed Pudding with Berries 56
Breakfast Tacos with Scrambled Tofu 57

SMOOTHIE RECIPES **58**

Blueberry Banana Smoothie 58
Green Power Smoothie 59
Berry Blast Smoothie 59
Peanut Butter Banana Smoothie 60
Mango Coconut Smoothie 61
Chocolate Peanut Butter Smoothie 62
Kale and Pineapple Smoothie 63
Tropical Green Smoothie 64
Apple Cinnamon Smoothie 65
Strawberry Banana Smoothie 66
Cherry Vanilla Smoothie 66
Orange Creamsicle Smoothie 67
Coffee Banana Smoothie 67
Raspberry Lemonade Smoothie 68
Peach Mango Smoothie 69

Almond Butter Banana Smoothie 69

Pina Colada Smoothie 70

Carrot Cake Smoothie 71

Watermelon Lime Smoothie 72

Spinach and Mango Smoothie 73

LUNCH RECIPES **74**

Overnight oats with berries and almonds   Ingredients: 74

Scrambled eggs with spinach and feta cheese 75

Greek yogurt with honey and sliced banana 75

Veggie omelette with mushrooms and peppers 77

Whole grain toast with avocado and smoked salmon   Ingredients: 78

Blueberry and chia seed smoothie bowl 78

Apple and cinnamon baked oatmeal 79

Cottage cheese and fresh fruit salad 80

Almond butter and banana on whole grain toast 80

Green smoothie with kale and pineapple 81

Mushroom and spinach frittata 82

Chia pudding with berries 83

Banana and almond butter smoothie 84

Sweet potato and black bean breakfast bowl 85

Quinoa breakfast bowl with fruit and nuts 86

Quinoa breakfast bowl with fruit and nuts 86

Egg and vegetable muffins 87

Berry and yogurt smoothie 88

Avocado and egg breakfast sandwich 88

Spinach and mushroom breakfast wrap 89

SNACK RECIPES **90**

Baked Sweet Potato Chips 90

Peanut Butter and Banana Bites 91

Roasted Chickpeas 92

Spicy Edamame 93

Greek Yogurt and Berry Parfait 94

Ants on a Log (Celery Sticks with Peanut Butter and Raisins) 95

Mini Caprese Skewers ... 96
Cucumber and Hummus Bites ... 96
Apple and Almond Butter Sandwiches ... 97
Quinoa and Veggie Stuffed Mini Peppers ... 98
Egg Salad Lettuce Wraps ... 99
Zucchini Pizza Bites Ingredients: ... 100
Chocolate Covered Strawberries ... 101
Trail Mix (Nuts, Seeds, and Dried Fruit) ... 102
Baked Kale Chips ... 103
Cottage Cheese and Pineapple Skewers ... 104
Grilled Shrimp Skewers ... 105
Almond Flour Crackers with Guacamole ... 106
Tuna Salad Cucumber Boats ... 107
Roasted Red Pepper and Feta Dip with Veggie Sticks ... 108

DINNER RECIPES ... 109

Baked Salmon with Roasted Vegetables ... 109
Grilled Chicken with Sweet Potato Mash ... 110
Beef and Broccoli Stir Fry ... 111
Spicy Shrimp Tacos with Avocado Salsa ... 112
Veggie and Quinoa Stuffed Peppers ... 113
Turkey Meatballs with Zucchini Noodles ... 114
Lemon Garlic Chicken with Asparagus ... 115
Cilantro Lime Shrimp with Cauliflower Rice ... 116
Pork Tenderloin with Apple Cranberry Chutney ... 117
Mushroom and Spinach Risotto ... 118
BBQ Chicken with Roasted Brussel Sprouts ... 119
Stuffed Butternut Squash with Quinoa and Kale ... 119
Tuna Salad Lettuce Wraps ... 121
Grilled Steak with Chimichurri Sauce ... 121
Sweet Potato and Black Bean Chili ... 123
Sesame Ginger Salmon with Broccoli ... 124
Eggplant Rollatini ... 125
Spicy Sausage and Kale Soup ... 126

    Baked Cod with Lemon and Herbs 127

    Cauliflower Crust Pizza with Pesto and Vegetables 127

DESSERT RECIPES **129**

    Chia Seed Pudding 129

    Mixed Berry Smoothie Bowl 130

    Banana Oat Cookies 131

    Chocolate Avocado Mousse 132

    Peanut Butter Banana Bites 132

    Mixed Fruit Salad 133

    Apple Cinnamon Oat Bars 134

    Vanilla Bean Greek Yogurt Popsicles 135

    Mixed Berry Cobbler 135

    Coconut Mango Popsicles 136

    Blueberry Lemon Cake Bars 137

    Peach Oatmeal Bars 138

    Chocolate Dipped Strawberries 139

    Raspberry Chia Jam 139

    Cinnamon Apple Chips 140

    Pumpkin Spice Energy Balls 141

    Strawberry Shortcake 142

    Lemon Blueberry Cheesecake Bars 143

    Carrot Cake Muffins 144

    Blackberry Coconut Pudding 145

Review This Book 146

Chapter 1: Introduction to Noom Diet Meal Prep

1.1 The Noom Diet Explained

The Noom Diet is more than just a weight loss plan; it's a lifestyle change that focuses on healthy eating habits and long-term results. The Noom Diet app, developed by a team of nutritionists and behavioral psychologists, uses a unique color-coding system to classify foods into three categories: green, yellow, and red. The goal is to help users make better food choices, develop portion control, and understand the impact of their eating habits on their overall health.

1.2 The Importance of Meal Prep in Your Noom Diet Journey

Meal prep is a crucial part of maintaining a healthy lifestyle, and it's especially important when following the Noom Diet. Preparing meals in advance can help you:

Save time during the week by reducing the need for daily cooking

Control portion sizes to avoid overeating

Maintain a balanced diet by including a variety of nutrient-dense foods

Resist the temptation of unhealthy, processed foods

Save money by reducing food waste and avoiding impulsive takeout orders

By incorporating meal prep into your Noom Diet journey, you can ensure that you have nutritious, Noom-approved meals ready to go, even on your busiest days.

1.3 Setting Up Your Kitchen for Success

Before diving into meal prep, it's essential to set up your kitchen for success. Here are some tips to help you get started:

Invest in high-quality, airtight food storage containers. Glass containers are an eco-friendly and durable option.

Organize your refrigerator and pantry to make it easy to find ingredients and keep track of inventory.

Stock up on essential kitchen tools such as a food scale, measuring cups, and spoons to ensure accuracy when portioning your meals.

Create a designated meal prep space in your kitchen to make the process more efficient and enjoyable.

Now that you have a better understanding of the Noom Diet and the importance of meal prep, it's time to dive into the practical aspects of incorporating this lifestyle change into your routine. In the following chapters, you'll learn how to stock your pantry, understand the Noom Diet color-coding system, and discover delicious meal prep ideas for breakfast, lunch, dinner, and snacks. With these tools at your disposal, you'll be well-equipped to embark on your Noom Diet journey and achieve lasting success.

Chapter 2: Stocking Your Pantry for Noom Diet Meal Prep

2.1 Essential Noom Diet Ingredients

To make Noom Diet meal prep a breeze, it's essential to have a well-stocked pantry with Noom-approved ingredients. Here are some staples to keep on hand:

Whole grains: Brown rice, quinoa, whole wheat pasta, oats, and barley
Legumes: Lentils, chickpeas, black beans, and kidney beans
Fruits and vegetables: Fresh, frozen, or canned (with no added sugar or salt)
Lean proteins: Chicken, turkey, fish, tofu, tempeh, and eggs
Nuts and seeds: Almonds, walnuts, chia seeds, and flaxseeds
Dairy or dairy alternatives: Greek yogurt, cottage cheese, almond milk, and soy milk
Healthy fats: Olive oil, avocado oil, and nut butters
Herbs and spices: Basil, cilantro, oregano, cumin, and paprika
Condiments and sauces: Low-sodium soy sauce, balsamic vinegar, and Dijon mustard

2.2 Creating a Noom-Friendly Shopping List

Having a shopping list is essential for staying on track with the Noom Diet. Use the Noom app to identify the foods you enjoy and the meals you want to prepare for the week. Divide your list into sections based on food categories, such as produce, proteins, and grains, to make your shopping trip more efficient.

Remember to include a variety of green, yellow, and red foods to ensure a balanced diet. When shopping, choose whole, minimally processed foods, and prioritize fresh, seasonal produce whenever possible.

2.3 Organizing Your Pantry for Noom Meal Prep

An organized pantry can make your Noom Diet meal prep much more manageable. Follow these steps to create a functional, Noom-friendly pantry:

Clear out any unhealthy, processed foods that do not align with the Noom Diet principles.
Group similar items together, such as grains, legumes, and canned goods, to make them easy to find.
Store frequently used items at eye level and less frequently used items on higher or lower shelves.
Label containers and shelves to help you quickly identify and locate ingredients.
Keep a running inventory of your pantry items to ensure you never run out of essential ingredients.
With a well-stocked and organized pantry, you'll be better equipped to tackle your Noom Diet meal prep and stay on track throughout the week.

In the next chapter, we'll explore the Noom Diet's color-coding system, focusing on green foods and how to incorporate them into your meal prep. By understanding the importance of each food category and learning how to make the most of these nutritious ingredients, you'll be well on your way to a healthier, happier lifestyle.

Chapter 3: Green Foods: The Foundation of the Noom Diet

3.1 Understanding Green Foods

Green foods are the cornerstone of the Noom Diet, as they are nutrient-dense and low in calories. They include fruits, vegetables, whole grains, and legumes, which are packed with essential vitamins, minerals, and fiber. The Noom Diet encourages you to fill the majority of your plate with green foods, as they promote satiety and provide long-lasting energy.

3.2 Top Green Foods for Meal Prep

Some green foods are particularly well-suited for meal prep, as they retain their freshness and nutrients when stored for several days. Here are some excellent green food options for meal prep:

Leafy greens: Spinach, kale, and collard greens
Cruciferous vegetables: Broccoli, cauliflower, and Brussels sprouts
Root vegetables: Sweet potatoes, carrots, and beets
Whole grains: Quinoa, brown rice, and farro
Legumes: Lentils, chickpeas, and black beans
Fruits: Berries, apples, and oranges

3.3 Green Foods Recipes for a Busy Week

Incorporating green foods into your meal prep is essential for staying on track with the Noom Diet. Here are some simple and delicious green food recipes you can prepare in advance:

Quinoa Salad with Roasted Vegetables
Cook quinoa according to package instructions and let it cool.
Roast a mix of your favorite vegetables, such as zucchini, bell peppers, and red onions, in the oven with a drizzle of olive oil and your choice of herbs and spices.
Combine the quinoa and roasted vegetables in a large bowl.
Add a handful of chopped fresh herbs, such as parsley or cilantro, and mix well.
Divide the salad into individual containers and store in the refrigerator for up to 4 days.
Lentil Soup with Kale and Sweet Potatoes
In a large pot, sauté diced onion, carrot, and celery in olive oil until softened.
Add minced garlic, diced sweet potatoes, and dried lentils, then stir to combine.
Pour in vegetable broth and bring the mixture to a boil.
Reduce heat and simmer until the lentils and sweet potatoes are tender.
Stir in chopped kale and cook until wilted.
Season with salt and pepper to taste, and let the soup cool before transferring to airtight containers.
Store in the refrigerator for up to 5 days or freeze for longer storage.
Fruit and Yogurt Parfaits
Layer Greek yogurt, your choice of fresh or frozen fruit, and a sprinkle of granola in individual jars or containers.
Top with a drizzle of honey or a handful of nuts for added crunch.
Store in the refrigerator for up to 3 days.

By filling your meal prep menu with green foods, you'll ensure that you're consuming nutrient-dense, satisfying meals that support your Noom Diet goals. In the following chapters, we'll explore the role of yellow and red foods in the Noom Diet and share more meal prep ideas to help you maintain a balanced and enjoyable eating plan.

Chapter 4: Yellow Foods: Moderation is Key

4.1 The Role of Yellow Foods in the Noom Diet

Yellow foods are those with moderate calorie density and somewhat lower nutrient content compared to green foods. They typically include lean proteins, starches, and some dairy products. While they are not as nutrient-dense as green foods, yellow foods still play a crucial role in a balanced diet by providing essential nutrients, such as protein and healthy fats. The Noom Diet encourages you to enjoy yellow foods in moderation, being mindful of portion sizes.

4.2 Incorporating Yellow Foods in Your Meal Prep

Including yellow foods in your meal prep helps create well-rounded meals that provide a mix of essential nutrients. Here are some tips for incorporating yellow foods in your Noom Diet meal prep:

Pair yellow foods with green foods to boost the nutrient content of your meals. For example, serve grilled chicken (yellow) with a side of steamed vegetables (green).
Use portion control when preparing yellow foods. Measure out servings of foods like pasta, rice, or cheese to ensure you don't overindulge.
Opt for healthier cooking methods, such as baking, grilling, or steaming, to avoid adding unnecessary calories to yellow foods.

4.3 Delicious Yellow Food Recipes

Try these tasty and Noom-approved yellow food recipes to add variety and flavor to your meal prep:

Baked Lemon Herb Chicken

Season boneless, skinless chicken breasts with a blend of lemon zest, minced garlic, dried herbs (such as thyme, rosemary, and oregano), salt, and pepper.

Bake the chicken in a preheated oven until cooked through.

Let the chicken cool, then slice or shred it for use in salads, wraps, or grain bowls throughout the week.

Whole Wheat Pasta Salad

Cook whole wheat pasta according to package instructions and let it cool.

Combine the pasta with chopped vegetables, such as bell peppers, cherry tomatoes, cucumber, and red onion.

Toss the pasta salad with a light vinaigrette made from olive oil, red wine vinegar, and a touch of Dijon mustard.

Store the pasta salad in the refrigerator for up to 4 days.

Overnight Oats with Almond Butter and Banana

In a jar or container, mix rolled oats with almond milk, a scoop of almond butter, and a touch of honey or maple syrup.

Top with sliced banana and a sprinkle of chia seeds.

Cover and refrigerate overnight or for up to 3 days.

Incorporating yellow foods into your Noom Diet meal prep ensures your meals are not only nutritious but also satisfying and delicious. In the next chapter, we'll discuss red foods and how to indulge mindfully while staying on track with your Noom Diet goals.

Chapter 5: Red Foods: Indulging Mindfully

5.1 Understanding Red Foods

Red foods are those with the highest calorie density and lowest nutrient content in the Noom Diet color-coding system. They typically include processed foods, high-fat meats, and sugary treats. While red foods are not off-limits on the Noom Diet, they should be consumed in smaller quantities and less frequently than green and yellow foods. The key to enjoying red foods is to practice moderation and mindfulness.

5.2 Tips for Including Red Foods in Your Meal Prep

It's essential to strike a balance between indulging in your favorite red foods and maintaining a healthy diet. Here are some tips for incorporating red foods into your Noom Diet meal prep:

Plan for red food indulgences in advance, so they don't derail your progress. For example, include a small portion of dark chocolate or a scoop of your favorite full-fat ice cream as an occasional treat.

Opt for healthier versions of your favorite red foods, such as baked sweet potato fries instead of deep-fried french fries or homemade air-popped popcorn instead of store-bought buttered popcorn.

Practice portion control by pre-packaging red food treats in single-serving containers, so you're not tempted to overindulge.

5.3 Guilt-Free Red Food Recipes

Enjoy these guilt-free red food recipes that allow you to indulge mindfully while staying on track with your Noom Diet goals:

Baked Sweet Potato Fries

Preheat the oven and line a baking sheet with parchment paper.

Peel and slice sweet potatoes into thin, even strips.

Toss the sweet potato fries with a small amount of olive oil and your choice of spices, such as paprika, garlic powder, and salt.

Spread the fries in a single layer on the prepared baking sheet and bake until crispy and golden brown.

Let the fries cool, then portion them into individual containers for a delicious and satisfying side dish or snack.

Dark Chocolate and Nut Clusters

Melt a small amount of dark chocolate (at least 70% cocoa) in a microwave-safe bowl.

Stir in a mix of your favorite unsalted nuts, such as almonds, walnuts, and pecans.

Drop spoonfuls of the chocolate-nut mixture onto a parchment-lined baking sheet and refrigerate until set.

Once hardened, store the clusters in an airtight container for a portion-controlled sweet treat.

Greek Yogurt Ranch Dip

In a small bowl, mix together plain Greek yogurt, a packet of ranch seasoning, and a splash of milk to thin the consistency.

Portion the dip into individual containers and serve with fresh vegetables or whole-grain crackers for a healthier take on a classic snack.

By incorporating red foods mindfully and in moderation, you can enjoy your favorite indulgences without sacrificing your Noom Diet goals. As you continue your journey, remember that the Noom Diet is about developing a healthy relationship with food and learning to make balanced choices that support your long-term wellbeing.

Chapter 6: Meal Prep Strategies for Long Work Weeks and Busy Days

6.1 Embracing Batch Cooking and Freezing

Batch cooking and freezing are excellent strategies for staying on track with your Noom Diet during long work weeks and busy days. By dedicating a few hours on the weekend to preparing large quantities of food, you can have healthy, homemade meals ready to go throughout the week. Consider cooking and freezing meals such as soups, stews, casseroles, and stir-fries, as they can be easily portioned and reheated when needed.

6.2 Incorporating Slow Cooker and Instant Pot Meals

Slow cookers and Instant Pots are convenient appliances that can simplify meal prep and save time during busy weeks. Simply add your ingredients to the appliance in the morning, set the cooking time, and come home to a delicious, Noom-approved meal. Look for slow cooker and Instant Pot recipes that focus on green and yellow foods, such as vegetable stews, lean protein dishes, and whole grain-based meals.

6.3 Creating a Meal Prep Schedule

Developing a meal prep schedule can help you stay organized and on track with your Noom Diet goals. Here's a simple process to create a meal prep schedule:

Choose your meal prep day(s): Pick a day or two each week when you have the time to dedicate to meal prep. Weekends often work well for this purpose.

Plan your meals: Use the Noom app to find recipes that align with your dietary preferences and goals. Plan for breakfast, lunch, dinner, and snacks throughout the week.

Make a shopping list: Based on your meal plan, create a shopping list to ensure you have all the ingredients needed for your recipes.

Shop and prep: On your designated meal prep day(s), shop for groceries and then prepare your meals. Focus on efficiency by using multitasking techniques such as cooking grains while chopping vegetables or prepping proteins.

Store and enjoy: Portion your prepared meals into individual containers and store them in the refrigerator or freezer until needed.

6.4 Time-Saving Meal Prep Tips

Here are some additional time-saving tips for your Noom Diet meal prep:

Use pre-cut vegetables and fruits to save time on chopping and slicing.

Invest in a food processor to quickly and easily chop, grate, and slice ingredients.

Cook multiple dishes at once by utilizing your oven, stovetop, and countertop appliances simultaneously.

Keep a well-stocked pantry with Noom-approved staples to minimize last-minute grocery trips.

Double or triple recipes to create larger quantities of food for leftovers or freezing.
By implementing these meal prep strategies and time-saving tips, you can stay on track with your Noom Diet goals, even during your busiest weeks. With a bit of planning and organization, you'll be well-equipped to maintain a healthy, balanced lifestyle and continue making progress on your wellness journey.

Chapter 7: Customizing Your Meal Prep for Dietary Preferences and Allergies

7.1 Adapting Noom Recipes for Vegetarians and Vegans

The Noom Diet is easily adaptable for vegetarians and vegans. When customizing meal prep recipes, simply swap out animal-based proteins for plant-based alternatives. Some excellent plant-based protein sources include:

Legumes: Lentils, chickpeas, black beans, and kidney beans
Tofu and tempeh
Seitan
Edamame
Nuts and seeds: Almonds, walnuts, chia seeds, and flaxseeds
Additionally, replace dairy products with plant-based alternatives, such as almond milk, soy milk, or coconut yogurt.

7.2 Adjusting Recipes for Gluten-Free Diets

For those following a gluten-free diet, it's crucial to substitute gluten-containing grains with gluten-free alternatives in your Noom Diet meal prep. Consider using the following gluten-free grains and grain substitutes:

Brown rice and wild rice
Quinoa
Buckwheat
Millet
Amaranth
Gluten-free oats

When selecting packaged products, always check labels for gluten-free certification to ensure they meet your dietary requirements.

7.3 Managing Food Allergies and Sensitivities

To accommodate food allergies and sensitivities, make necessary adjustments to Noom Diet meal prep recipes. Here are some common food allergies and suggested alternatives:

Nut allergy: Replace nuts with seeds, such as sunflower seeds, pumpkin seeds, or sesame seeds, for added crunch and healthy fats.

Soy allergy: Opt for alternative protein sources, such as legumes or gluten-free grains, and use coconut aminos instead of soy sauce.

Dairy allergy: Choose plant-based milk and yogurt alternatives, and replace cheese with nutritional yeast or dairy-free cheese substitutes.

When planning your meal prep, be sure to customize recipes according to your specific dietary needs and preferences. The Noom app can also help you find suitable alternatives and adjustments for your unique requirements.

7.4 Creating a Balanced and Personalized Meal Plan

The key to a successful Noom Diet meal prep is creating a balanced and personalized meal plan that takes your dietary preferences and allergies into account. Use the Noom app to search for recipes that cater to your specific needs, and don't be afraid to get creative with substitutions and adjustments.

Remember to focus on green and yellow foods, while enjoying red foods in moderation. By customizing your meal plan and meal prep to suit your preferences and dietary requirements, you'll be well on your way to maintaining a healthy, balanced lifestyle with the Noom Diet.

Chapter 8: Staying Motivated and Overcoming Meal Prep Obstacles

8.1 Identifying Common Meal Prep Challenges

Maintaining motivation and overcoming obstacles are critical aspects of successful meal prep. Some common challenges include:

Boredom with repetitive meals
Time constraints
Limited access to fresh ingredients
Lack of culinary skills or creativity
By acknowledging these challenges, you can develop strategies to overcome them and stay on track with your Noom Diet meal prep goals.

8.2 Keeping Your Meal Prep Fresh and Exciting

To avoid boredom and maintain motivation, aim to keep your meal prep fresh and exciting. Consider the following tips:

Rotate your meal plan: Avoid eating the same meals every week by rotating your meal plan and incorporating a variety of different recipes.
Experiment with new ingredients: Broaden your culinary horizons by trying new fruits, vegetables, grains, and proteins.

Use different cooking techniques: Explore various cooking methods, such as grilling, roasting, steaming, or stir-frying, to add variety to your meal prep.

Get inspired by international cuisines: Take inspiration from global flavors and cuisines, such as Mediterranean, Mexican, Asian, or Indian dishes, to bring excitement and diversity to your meals.

8.3 Time Management Strategies for Meal Prep

Time constraints can be a significant obstacle for many people when it comes to meal prep. Here are some tips for managing your time effectively:

Plan ahead: Create a detailed meal plan and shopping list to streamline your grocery shopping and meal prep process.

Use time-saving tools: Invest in kitchen gadgets and appliances that can save time, such as food processors, slow cookers, and Instant Pots.

Multi-task in the kitchen: Cook multiple dishes simultaneously to make the most of your meal prep time. For example, roast vegetables while cooking grains or preparing a protein dish.

Utilize pre-prepared ingredients: Consider using pre-chopped vegetables, pre-cooked grains, or canned beans to save time during your meal prep.

8.4 Building Culinary Confidence

Developing culinary skills and confidence is essential for successful meal prep. To enhance your abilities in the kitchen:

Learn from online resources: Explore cooking blogs, YouTube channels, or online courses to learn new techniques, recipes, and culinary skills.

Practice regularly: The more you cook, the more confident and skilled you will become in the kitchen.

Start with simple recipes: Begin with easy, no-fuss recipes that require minimal ingredients and steps, then gradually progress to more complex dishes.

Seek support from the Noom community: Connect with fellow Noom users to exchange tips, recipes, and encouragement, helping you build confidence in your meal prep journey.

By addressing these common meal prep obstacles and staying motivated, you can maintain a consistent and enjoyable Noom Diet meal prep routine that supports your long-term health and wellness goals.

Chapter 9: Meal Prep for Weight Loss Plateaus and Maintaining Progress

9.1 Navigating Weight Loss Plateaus

Weight loss plateaus are common during any weight loss journey, including when following the Noom Diet. They occur when your body adapts to the changes you've made and weight loss slows down or stops. To overcome a weight loss plateau, it's essential to reassess your meal prep and make adjustments as needed.

9.2 Strategies for Overcoming Plateaus with Meal Prep

Here are some strategies to help you overcome a weight loss plateau while staying on track with your Noom Diet meal prep:

Reevaluate portion sizes: Double-check your portion sizes and ensure you're not consuming larger servings than necessary, especially with yellow and red foods.

Adjust macronutrient balance: Assess your macronutrient balance, focusing on incorporating more green foods, lean proteins, and complex carbohydrates while minimizing processed and high-fat foods.

Incorporate more whole foods: Emphasize whole, unprocessed foods in your meal prep to increase nutrient density and minimize empty calories.

Monitor your snacking habits: Be mindful of snacking between meals, as it can contribute to excess calorie intake. Opt for nutrient-dense, low-calorie snacks, such as fresh fruits, vegetables, or a handful of nuts.

Stay hydrated: Ensure you're drinking enough water throughout the day, as proper hydration is essential for overall health and weight loss.

9.3 Maintaining Your Progress with Meal Prep

Once you've reached your weight loss goals, it's crucial to maintain your progress by continuing your meal prep routine. Use the following tips to stay on track and maintain your achievements:

Set new goals: Transition from weight loss goals to maintenance or fitness goals to maintain motivation and focus on long-term health.

Continue to track your meals: Use the Noom app to track your meals and ensure you're staying within your maintenance calorie range.

Stay consistent with meal prep: Stick to your meal prep schedule to avoid falling back into unhealthy eating habits and to maintain your progress.

Make adjustments as needed: As your needs and lifestyle change, be prepared to adjust your meal plan and meal prep accordingly.

Stay connected with the Noom community: Continue to engage with the Noom community for support, motivation, and accountability.

By addressing weight loss plateaus and focusing on maintaining your progress, you can ensure that your Noom Diet meal prep routine continues to support your long-term health and wellness goals. Remember, the key to success is consistency and persistence, as well as adapting to your changing needs and circumstances.

Chapter 10: Incorporating Exercise and Mindfulness into Your Noom Diet Journey

10.1 The Importance of Exercise

While meal prep and a balanced diet are essential components of the Noom Diet, exercise plays a crucial role in promoting overall health and accelerating weight loss. Engaging in regular physical activity not only helps you burn calories but also improves cardiovascular health, increases energy levels, and enhances mental wellbeing.

10.2 Finding the Right Exercise Routine

To create a sustainable exercise routine that complements your Noom Diet meal prep, consider the following tips:

Choose activities you enjoy: Select exercises and activities that you genuinely enjoy, as you'll be more likely to stick to a routine if it's something you look forward to.
Set realistic goals: Establish achievable fitness goals that are tailored to your current fitness level and schedule.
Mix it up: Incorporate a variety of exercises into your routine, including cardio, strength training, and flexibility exercises, to keep it interesting and engaging.
Find a workout buddy or group: Exercising with a friend or joining a workout group can provide motivation, accountability, and social interaction.

10.3 Mindfulness and the Noom Diet

Mindfulness is an essential aspect of the Noom Diet approach, as it encourages a healthy relationship with food and self-awareness. Practicing mindfulness can help you recognize and manage emotional eating, improve portion control, and enhance overall wellbeing.

10.4 Incorporating Mindfulness Techniques into Your Routine

Incorporate the following mindfulness techniques into your daily routine to support your Noom Diet meal prep and weight loss journey:

Mindful eating: Take the time to savor each bite, focusing on the flavors, textures, and aromas of your food. Eat slowly and without distractions to develop a greater awareness of your hunger and fullness cues.

Meditation: Dedicate a few minutes each day to practice meditation, focusing on your breath and bringing awareness to your thoughts and feelings without judgment.

Gratitude journaling: Record daily reflections on things you're grateful for, helping you cultivate a positive mindset and appreciate the progress you've made in your Noom Diet journey.

Body awareness exercises: Engage in gentle body awareness exercises, such as yoga or tai chi, to increase your connection with your body and improve your overall sense of wellbeing.

By incorporating exercise and mindfulness practices into your Noom Diet journey, you'll create a well-rounded, holistic approach to weight loss and wellness that extends beyond meal prep and nutrition. Embracing these practices can help you maintain long-term success, improved mental and physical health, and a more balanced lifestyle.

Chapter 11: Making the Noom Diet a Sustainable Lifestyle Choice

11.1 The Importance of Sustainability

To experience lasting success with the Noom Diet, it's essential to view it as a sustainable lifestyle choice rather than a temporary fix. By developing healthy habits and routines around meal prep, exercise, and mindfulness, you can maintain your progress, avoid the pitfalls of yo-yo dieting, and continue to prioritize your health and wellbeing.

11.2 Long-Term Meal Prep Strategies

To ensure that your Noom Diet meal prep remains sustainable, consider the following long-term strategies:

Be flexible: Allow yourself the flexibility to adjust your meal plan and meal prep based on your evolving needs, preferences, and circumstances.

Maintain variety: Continuously explore new recipes, ingredients, and cooking techniques to prevent boredom and keep your meal prep fresh and engaging.

Share your journey: Involve family and friends in your Noom Diet meal prep by sharing recipes, cooking together, or discussing your progress and challenges.

Reflect on your progress: Periodically review your achievements and challenges to identify areas for improvement and celebrate your successes.

11.3 Balancing Indulgences with Healthy Choices

A sustainable Noom Diet lifestyle involves finding a balance between indulgences and healthy choices. Rather than completely restricting yourself from treats, practice moderation and plan for occasional indulgences within your meal prep. This approach can help prevent feelings of deprivation and support long-term adherence to the Noom Diet.

11.4 Staying Accountable and Supported

Accountability and support are vital for maintaining a sustainable Noom Diet lifestyle. Stay connected with the Noom community, engage with friends and family, and consider seeking professional guidance from a coach or nutritionist if needed. By surrounding yourself with a supportive network, you'll be better equipped to handle challenges and stay motivated in your Noom Diet journey.

11.5 Embracing a Holistic Approach to Wellness

A sustainable Noom Diet lifestyle goes beyond meal prep and nutrition. It encompasses a holistic approach to wellness, including regular exercise, mindfulness practices, and self-care. By nurturing all aspects of your health and wellbeing, you can cultivate a balanced and fulfilling lifestyle that supports your long-term goals.

By focusing on sustainability and embracing a holistic approach to the Noom Diet, you can turn your meal prep routine and healthy habits into a lasting lifestyle choice. This commitment to your health and wellbeing will not only support your weight loss goals but also enhance your overall quality of life.

Chapter 12: Celebrating Your Success and Planning for the Future

12.1 Acknowledging Your Achievements

As you progress in your Noom Diet journey, it's essential to celebrate your successes, both big and small. Acknowledging your achievements can boost your motivation and help you maintain a positive mindset. Take the time to reflect on the progress you've made, including improvements in your eating habits, weight loss, physical fitness, and overall wellbeing.

12.2 Setting New Health and Wellness Goals

Once you've reached your initial weight loss and health goals, consider setting new objectives to continue challenging yourself and growing. New goals can include:

Fitness-related targets, such as running a 5K or increasing your strength
Nutritional objectives, like incorporating more plant-based meals or reducing added sugars
Mindfulness and stress management goals, such as developing a daily meditation practice or improving work-life balance
Self-care and personal development goals, like exploring new hobbies or prioritizing quality time with loved ones

12.3 Adapting Your Noom Diet Meal Prep to Evolving Needs

As your goals and lifestyle change, it's crucial to adapt your Noom Diet meal prep accordingly. For example, if you begin training for a marathon, you may need to adjust your meal plan to include more carbohydrates and calories. Continuously reassess your meal prep routine to ensure it supports your current objectives and lifestyle.

Maintaining Your Wellness Goals

12.4 Lifelong Learning and Growth

Embrace a mindset of lifelong learning and growth by continually seeking new knowledge and skills related to health, nutrition, and wellness. Stay curious and open to new ideas, and never hesitate to ask questions, seek support, or explore new resources. By staying informed and engaged in your Noom Diet journey, you'll continue to grow and make progress in all aspects of your health and wellbeing.

12.5 Inspiring Others with Your Success

Lastly, consider sharing your Noom Diet success story with others to inspire and support those beginning their own health and wellness journeys. By offering encouragement, advice, and personal insights, you can help others navigate the challenges and triumphs of their own Noom Diet experiences.

In conclusion, the Noom Diet meal prep journey is a transformative process that can support lasting weight loss, improved health, and a sustainable lifestyle. By celebrating your successes, setting new goals, adapting to your evolving needs, and inspiring others, you can continue to thrive in your Noom Diet journey and enjoy a lifetime of health and wellness.

BREAKFAST RECIPES

Green Smoothie Bowl

Ingredients:

- 1 cup spinach
- 1/2 avocado
- 1/2 banana
- 1/2 cup almond milk
- 1/2 cup ice
- Toppings: sliced almonds, chia seeds, and fresh berries

Instructions:

1. In a blender, combine spinach, avocado, banana, almond milk, and ice. Blend until smooth.
2. Pour into a bowl and top with sliced almonds, chia seeds, and fresh berries.

Overnight Chia Pudding with Berries

Ingredients:

- 1/4 cup chia seeds
- 1 cup almond milk
- 1/2 tsp vanilla extract
- 1 tbsp honey or maple syrup
- 1/2 cup fresh berries

Instructions:

1. In a jar or container, mix chia seeds, almond milk, vanilla extract, and honey or maple syrup.
2. Cover and refrigerate overnight.
3. In the morning, stir the pudding and top with fresh berries.

Veggie Egg White Scramble

Ingredients:

- 1 cup chopped vegetables (e.g., bell peppers, onions, tomatoes)
- 1/2 cup egg whites
- 1 tbsp olive oil
- Salt and pepper, to taste

Instructions:

1. Heat olive oil in a skillet over medium heat. Add chopped vegetables and sauté until softened.
2. Add egg whites, salt, and pepper. Cook, stirring occasionally, until eggs are cooked through.

Greek Yogurt Parfait with Fresh Fruit and Granola

Ingredients:

- 1 cup Greek yogurt
- 1/2 cup fresh fruit (e.g., berries, sliced banana)
- 1/4 cup granola

Instructions:

1. In a glass or bowl, layer Greek yogurt, fresh fruit, and granola. Serve immediately.

Protein-Packed Quinoa Porridge

Ingredients:

- 1/2 cup cooked quinoa
- 1/2 cup almond milk
- 1 tbsp honey or maple syrup
- 1/2 tsp cinnamon
- Toppings: chopped nuts, dried fruit, and a drizzle of honey or maple syrup

Instructions:

1. In a saucepan, combine cooked quinoa, almond milk, honey or maple syrup, and cinnamon. Cook over medium heat, stirring occasionally, until heated through.
2. Transfer to a bowl and top with chopped nuts, dried fruit, and an additional drizzle of honey or maple syrup.

Banana Oat Pancakes

Ingredients:

- 1 ripe banana, mashed
- 1 cup rolled oats
- 1/2 cup milk (dairy or non-dairy)
- 1 egg
- 1/2 tsp baking powder
- 1/2 tsp cinnamon
- 1/4 tsp salt
- Cooking spray or oil for the pan

Instructions:

1. In a blender, combine all ingredients and blend until smooth.
2. Heat a non-stick skillet or griddle over medium heat and lightly coat with cooking spray or oil.
3. Pour 1/4 cup of batter onto the skillet for each pancake. Cook until bubbles form on the surface, then flip and cook until golden brown.

Smoked Salmon and Avocado Toast

Ingredients:

- 2 slices whole-grain bread, toasted
- 1/2 avocado, mashed
- 3 oz smoked salmon
- Salt and pepper, to taste
- Optional: thinly sliced red onion, capers, and fresh dill

Instructions:

1. Spread mashed avocado onto the toasted bread.
2. Top with smoked salmon, salt, and pepper. If desired
3. The previous model used in this conversation is unavailable. We've switched you to the latest default model add thinly sliced red onion, capers, and fresh dill.

Spinach and Feta Egg Muffins

Ingredients:

- 6 eggs
- 1/4 cup milk (dairy or non-dairy)
- 1/2 cup chopped spinach
- 1/4 cup crumbled feta cheese
- Salt and pepper, to taste

Instructions:

1. Preheat the oven to 350°F (175°C). Grease a muffin tin.
2. In a bowl, whisk together eggs and milk. Stir in chopped spinach and feta cheese. Add salt and pepper to taste.
3. Pour the mixture evenly into the muffin cups.
4. Bake for 18-20 minutes, or until the egg muffins are set and slightly golden on top.

Almond Butter and Apple Rice Cake

Ingredients:

- 1 rice cake
- 1 tbsp almond butter
- 1/2 apple, thinly sliced
- 1 tsp honey

Instructions:

1. Spread almond butter onto the rice cake.
2. Top with thinly sliced apple.
3. Drizzle honey over the top.

Mixed Berry Protein Smoothie

Ingredients:

- 1 cup mixed berries (fresh or frozen)
- 1/2 cup Greek yogurt
- 1/2 cup almond milk
- 1 scoop vanilla protein powder (optional)
- 1/2 cup ice

Instructions:

1. In a blender, combine mixed berries, Greek yogurt, almond milk, protein powder (if using), and ice. Blend until smooth.

Cauliflower Hash Browns with Salsa

Ingredients:

- 2 cups cauliflower rice
- 1/4 cup almond flour
- 1 egg
- 1/2 tsp garlic powder
- 1/2 tsp onion powder
- Salt and pepper, to taste
- Cooking spray or oil for the pan
- Salsa, for serving

Instructions:

1. In a bowl, combine cauliflower rice, almond flour, egg, garlic powder, onion powder, salt, and pepper.
2. Heat a non-stick skillet over medium heat and lightly coat with cooking spray or oil.
3. Spoon the cauliflower mixture into the skillet, forming small hash browns. Cook for 3-4 minutes on each side, until golden brown.
4. Serve with salsa.

Whole Wheat Breakfast Burrito with Black Beans

Ingredients:

- 1 whole wheat tortilla
- 1/2 cup black beans
- 2 eggs, scrambled
- 1/4 cup shredded cheddar cheese
- 1/4 cup salsa
- Salt and pepper, to taste

Instructions:

1. Heat the tortilla in the microwave or on a skillet until warm.
2. In a bowl, combine black beans, scrambled eggs, shredded cheddar cheese, salsa, salt, and pepper.
3. Spoon the mixture onto the tortilla and wrap it up.

Zucchini and Tomato Frittata

Ingredients:

- 4 eggs
- 1/4 cup milk (dairy or non-dairy)
- 1 small zucchini, sliced
- 1 small tomato, chopped
- 1/4 cup crumbled feta cheese
- 1 tbsp olive oil
- Salt and pepper, to taste

Instructions:

1. Preheat the oven to 350°F (175°C).
2. In a bowl, whisk together eggs and milk. Add salt and pepper to taste.
3. In an oven-safe skillet, heat olive oil over medium heat. Add sliced zucchini and chopped tomato and sauté until softened.
4. Pour the egg mixture into the skillet and sprinkle with crumbled feta cheese
5. . Transfer the skillet to the preheated oven and bake for 12-15 minutes, or until the frittata is set and slightly golden on top.

Peanut Butter and Banana Smoothie

Ingredients:

- 1 ripe banana
- 1 tbsp peanut butter
- 1/2 cup Greek yogurt
- 1/2 cup almond milk
- 1/2 cup ice

Instructions:

1. In a blender, combine banana, peanut butter, Greek yogurt, almond milk, and ice. Blend until smooth.

Sweet Potato and Kale Breakfast Hash

Ingredients:

- 1 sweet potato, diced
- 2 cups chopped kale
- 1/4 cup chopped onion
- 1/4 cup chopped red bell pepper
- 1 tbsp olive oil
- Salt and pepper, to taste
- 2 eggs

Instructions:

1. In a skillet, heat olive oil over medium heat. Add sweet potato, chopped kale, chopped onion, and chopped red bell pepper. Cook, stirring occasionally, until sweet potato is softened and slightly browned.
2. Push the vegetable mixture to the side of the skillet and crack 2 eggs into the empty space. Cook until the eggs are cooked to your liking.
3. Season with salt and pepper.

Blueberry Protein Muffins

Ingredients:

- 1 cup almond flour
- 1/4 cup vanilla protein powder
- 1/2 tsp baking soda
- 1/4 tsp salt
- 2 eggs
- 1/4 cup maple syrup
- 1/4 cup almond milk
- 1 tsp vanilla extract
- 1/2 cup blueberries

Instructions:

1. Preheat the oven to 350°F (175°C). Grease a muffin tin.
2. In a bowl, whisk together almond flour, protein powder, baking soda, and salt.
3. In a separate bowl, whisk together eggs, maple syrup, almond milk, and vanilla extract.
4. Add the dry ingredients to the wet ingredients and stir until well combined.
5. Fold in blueberries.
6. Pour the batter into the muffin cups.
7. Bake for 18-20 minutes, or until the muffins are golden brown and a toothpick inserted into the center comes out clean.

Avocado and Egg Toast

Ingredients:

- 1 slice whole-grain bread, toasted
- 1/2 avocado, mashed
- 1 egg, cooked to your liking
- Salt and pepper, to taste

Instructions:

1. Spread mashed avocado onto the toasted bread.
2. Top with a cooked egg.
3. Season with salt and pepper.

Oatmeal Breakfast Cookies

Ingredients:

- 1 1/2 cups rolled oats
- 1/2 cup almond flour
- 1/4 cup honey or maple syrup
- 1/4 cup coconut oil, melted
- 1 egg
- 1/2 tsp baking powder
- 1/2 tsp cinnamon
- 1/4 tsp salt
- 1/2 cup dried cranberries or raisins

Instructions:

1. Preheat the oven to 350°F (175°C). Line a baking sheet with parchment paper.
2. In a bowl, combine rolled oats, almond flour, honey or maple syrup, melted coconut oil, egg, baking powder, cinnamon, and salt. Stir until well combined.
3. Fold in dried cranberries or raisins.
4. Use a cookie scoop or spoon to drop the batter onto the prepared baking sheet, forming cookies.
5. Bake for 12-15 minutes, or until the cookies are golden brown and set.

Chia Seed Pudding with Berries

Ingredients:

- 1/4 cup chia seeds
- 1 cup almond milk
- 1 tsp honey or maple syrup
- 1/2 tsp vanilla extract
- 1/2 cup mixed berries

Instructions:

1. In a bowl, whisk together chia seeds, almond milk, honey or maple syrup, and vanilla extract. Let the mixture sit for at least 30 minutes, stirring occasionally, until it thickens to a pudding-like consistency.
2. Top with mixed berries.

Breakfast Tacos with Scrambled Tofu

Ingredients:

- 2 corn tortillas
- 1/2 block firm tofu, crumbled
- 1/4 cup chopped onion
- 1/4 cup chopped red bell pepper
- 1/4 cup chopped green bell pepper
- 1/4 cup salsa
- Salt and pepper, to taste

Instructions:

1. Heat the tortillas in the microwave or on a skillet until warm.
2. In a skillet, sauté crumbled tofu, chopped onion, chopped red bell pepper, and chopped green bell pepper until the vegetables are softened and the tofu is slightly browned.
3. Season with salt and pepper.
4. Spoon the tofu mixture onto the tortillas and top with salsa.

These 20 breakfast recipes are not only delicious, but also healthy and perfect for meal prepping. With this ultimate guide and cookbook, you'll be able to transform your life and stay on track with the Noom diet.

SMOOTHIE RECIPES

Blueberry Banana Smoothie

Ingredients:

- 1 banana
- 1 cup blueberries
- 1/2 cup plain Greek yogurt
- 1/2 cup unsweetened almond milk
- 1 tablespoon honey (optional)

Instructions:

1. Combine all ingredients in a blender and blend until smooth.
2. If the smoothie is too thick, add more almond milk until it reaches your desired consistency.
3. Serve and enjoy!

Green Power Smoothie

Ingredients:

- 1 banana
- 1 cup spinach
- 1/2 avocado
- 1/2 cup unsweetened almond milk
- 1/2 cup water
- 1 tablespoon honey (optional)

Instructions:

1. Combine all ingredients in a blender and blend until smooth.
2. If the smoothie is too thick, add more water until it reaches your desired consistency.
3. Serve and enjoy!

Berry Blast Smoothie

Ingredients:

- 1 banana
- 1/2 cup strawberries
- 1/2 cup blueberries
- 1/2 cup raspberries
- 1/2 cup unsweetened almond milk
- 1 tablespoon honey (optional)

Instructions:

1. Combine all ingredients in a blender and blend until smooth.
2. If the smoothie is too thick, add more almond milk until it reaches your desired consistency.
3. Serve and enjoy!

Peanut Butter Banana Smoothie

Ingredients:

- 1 banana
- 2 tablespoons peanut butter
- 1/2 cup plain Greek yogurt
- 1/2 cup unsweetened almond milk
- 1 tablespoon honey (optional)

Instructions:

1. Combine all ingredients in a blender and blend until smooth.
2. If the smoothie is too thick, add more almond milk until it reaches your desired consistency.
3. Serve and enjoy!

Mango Coconut Smoothie

Ingredients:

- 1 cup frozen mango chunks
- 1/2 cup coconut milk
- 1/2 cup unsweetened almond milk
- 1/2 cup plain Greek yogurt
- 1 tablespoon honey (optional)

Instructions:

1. Combine all ingredients in a blender and blend until smooth.
2. If the smoothie is too thick, add more almond milk until it reaches your desired consistency.
3. Serve and enjoy!

Chocolate Peanut Butter Smoothie

Ingredients:

- 1 banana
- 2 tablespoons peanut butter
- 1 tablespoon cocoa powder
- 1/2 cup unsweetened almond milk
- 1/2 cup plain Greek yogurt
- 1 tablespoon honey (optional)

Instructions:

1. Combine all ingredients in a blender and blend until smooth.
2. If the smoothie is too thick, add more almond milk until it reaches your desired consistency.
3. Serve and enjoy!

Kale and Pineapple Smoothie

Ingredients:

- 1 cup kale leaves, chopped
- 1 cup frozen pineapple chunks
- 1/2 cup unsweetened almond milk
- 1/2 cup water
- 1 tablespoon honey (optional)

Instructions:

1. Combine all ingredients in a blender and blend until smooth.
2. If the smoothie is too thick, add more water until it reaches your desired consistency.
3. Serve and enjoy!

Tropical Green Smoothie

Ingredients:

- 1 banana
- 1 cup spinach
- 1/2 cup frozen mango chunks
- 1/2 cup unsweetened almond milk
- 1/2 cup
- pineapple chunks
- 1 tablespoon honey (optional)

Instructions:

1. Combine all ingredients in a blender and blend until smooth.
2. If the smoothie is too thick, add more almond milk until it reaches your desired consistency.
3. Serve and enjoy!

Apple Cinnamon Smoothie

Ingredients:

- 1 apple, peeled and chopped
- 1/2 teaspoon cinnamon
- 1/2 cup plain Greek yogurt
- 1/2 cup unsweetened almond milk
- 1 tablespoon honey (optional)

Instructions:

1. Combine all ingredients in a blender and blend until smooth.
2. If the smoothie is too thick, add more almond milk until it reaches your desired consistency.
3. Serve and enjoy!

Strawberry Banana Smoothie

Ingredients:

- 1 banana
- 1/2 cup strawberries
- 1/2 cup plain Greek yogurt
- 1/2 cup unsweetened almond milk
- 1 tablespoon honey (optional)

Instructions:

1. Combine all ingredients in a blender and blend until smooth.
2. If the smoothie is too thick, add more almond milk until it reaches your desired consistency.
3. Serve and enjoy!

Cherry Vanilla Smoothie

Ingredients:

- 1 cup frozen cherries
- 1/2 cup plain Greek yogurt
- 1/2 cup unsweetened almond milk
- 1/2 teaspoon vanilla extract
- 1 tablespoon honey (optional)

Instructions:

1. Combine all ingredients in a blender and blend until smooth.

2. If the smoothie is too thick, add more almond milk until it reaches your desired consistency.
3. Serve and enjoy!

Orange Creamsicle Smoothie

Ingredients:

- 1 orange, peeled and segmented
- 1/2 cup plain Greek yogurt
- 1/2 cup unsweetened almond milk
- 1 tablespoon honey (optional)

Instructions:

1. Combine all ingredients in a blender and blend until smooth.
2. If the smoothie is too thick, add more almond milk until it reaches your desired consistency.
3. Serve and enjoy!

Coffee Banana Smoothie

Ingredients:

- 1 banana
- 1/2 cup brewed coffee, cooled
- 1/2 cup unsweetened almond milk
- 1/2 cup plain Greek yogurt
- 1 tablespoon honey (optional)

Instructions:

1. Combine all ingredients in a blender and blend until smooth.
2. If the smoothie is too thick, add more almond milk until it reaches your desired consistency.
3. Serve and enjoy!

Raspberry Lemonade Smoothie

Ingredients:

- 1 cup frozen raspberries
- 1/2 cup plain Greek yogurt
- 1/2 cup unsweetened almond milk
- 1/4 cup lemon juice
- 1 tablespoon honey (optional)

Instructions:

1. Combine all ingredients in a blender and blend until smooth.
2. If the smoothie is too thick, add more almond milk until it reaches your desired consistency.
3. Serve and enjoy!

Peach Mango Smoothie

Ingredients:

- 1 cup frozen peach slices
- 1/2 cup frozen mango chunks
- 1/2 cup unsweetened almond milk
- 1/2 cup plain Greek yogurt
- 1 tablespoon honey (optional)

Instructions:

1. Combine all ingredients in a blender and blend until smooth.
2. If the smoothie is too thick, add more almond milk until it reaches your desired consistency.
3. Serve and enjoy!

Almond Butter Banana Smoothie

Ingredients:

- 1 banana
- 2 tablespoons almond butter

continua

- 1/2 cup plain Greek yogurt
- 1/2 cup unsweetened almond milk
- 1 tablespoon honey (optional)

Instructions:

1. Combine all ingredients in a blender and blend until smooth.
2. If the smoothie is too thick, add more almond milk until it reaches your desired consistency.
3. Serve and enjoy!

Pina Colada Smoothie

Ingredients:

- 1 cup frozen pineapple chunks
- 1/2 cup coconut milk
- 1/2 cup unsweetened almond milk
- 1/2 cup plain Greek yogurt
- 1 tablespoon honey (optional)

Instructions:

1. Combine all ingredients in a blender and blend until smooth.
2. If the smoothie is too thick, add more almond milk until it reaches your desired consistency.
3. Serve and enjoy!

Carrot Cake Smoothie

Ingredients:

- 1 cup shredded carrots
- 1/2 teaspoon cinnamon
- 1/4 teaspoon nutmeg
- 1/2 cup unsweetened almond milk
- 1/2 cup plain Greek yogurt
- 1 tablespoon honey (optional)

Instructions:

1. Combine all ingredients in a blender and blend until smooth.
2. If the smoothie is too thick, add more almond milk until it reaches yourdesired consistency.
3. Serve and enjoy!

Watermelon Lime Smoothie

Ingredients:

- 1 cup cubed watermelon
- 1/4 cup lime juice
- 1/2 cup unsweetened almond milk
- 1/2 cup plain Greek yogurt
- 1 tablespoon honey (optional)

Instructions:

1. Combine all ingredients in a blender and blend until smooth.
2. If the smoothie is too thick, add more almond milk until it reaches your desired consistency.
3. Serve and enjoy!

Spinach and Mango Smoothie

Ingredients:

- 1 cup spinach leaves
- 1 cup frozen mango chunks
- 1/2 cup unsweetened almond milk
- 1/2 cup plain Greek yogurt
- 1 tablespoon honey (optional)

Instructions:

1. Combine all ingredients in a blender and blend until smooth.
2. If the smoothie is too thick, add more almond milk until it reaches your desired consistency.
3. Serve and enjoy!

LUNCH RECIPES

Overnight oats with berries and almonds

Ingredients:

- 1/2 cup rolled oats
- 1/2 cup unsweetened almond milk
- 1/2 cup mixed berries
- 1 tbsp honey
- 1 tbsp sliced almonds

Instructions:

- In a mason jar, mix together the rolled oats, almond milk, and honey.
- Add the mixed berries on top and sprinkle with sliced almonds.
- Seal the jar and refrigerate overnight.
- Serve cold in the morning.

Scrambled eggs with spinach and feta cheese

Ingredients:

- 2 eggs
- 1 cup fresh spinach
- 1/4 cup crumbled feta cheese
- Salt and pepper to taste

Instructions:

- In a non-stick pan, cook the spinach over medium heat until wilted.
- Crack the eggs into the pan and scramble with a spatula.
- Add the feta cheese and cook until melted.
- Season with salt and pepper to taste.

Greek yogurt with honey and sliced banana

Ingredients:

- 1 cup plain Greek yogurt
- 1 tbsp honey
- 1 banana, sliced

Instructions:

- In a bowl, mix together the Greek yogurt and honey.
- Top with sliced banana and enjoy!

Veggie omelette with mushrooms and peppers

Ingredients:

- 2 eggs
- 1/4 cup sliced mushrooms
- 1/4 cup diced peppers
- 1 tbsp olive oil
- Salt and pepper to taste

Instructions:

- In a non-stick pan, sauté the mushrooms and peppers in olive oil over medium heat until tender.
- Beat the eggs in a bowl and pour into the pan.
- Cook until set, then fold the omelette in half.
- Season with salt and pepper to taste.

Whole grain toast with avocado and smoked salmon

Ingredients:

- 1 slice whole grain bread
- 1/4 avocado, mashed
- 1 oz smoked salmon
- 1 tsp lemon juice

Instructions:

- Toast the bread and spread the mashed avocado on top.
- Add the smoked salmon and drizzle with lemon juice.

Blueberry and chia seed smoothie bowl

Ingredients:
- 1/2 cup frozen blueberries
- 1/2 banana
- 1/2 cup unsweetened almond milk
- 1 tbsp chia seeds
- 1 tbsp honey
- Toppings of your choice (granola, fresh fruit, etc.)

Instructions:

- In a blender, mix together the blueberries, banana, almond milk, chia seeds, and honey until smooth.
- Pour into a bowl and add your desired toppings.

Apple and cinnamon baked oatmeal

Ingredients:
- 1 cup rolled oats
- 1/2 tsp baking powder
- 1/2 tsp cinnamon
- 1/4 tsp salt
- 1 cup unsweetened almond milk
- 1 egg
- 1 apple, diced
- 1 tbsp honey

Instructions:
- Preheat the oven to 375°F.
- In a bowl, mix together the rolled oats, baking powder, cinnamon, and salt.
- In a separate bowl, whisk together the almond milk, egg, and honey.
- Stir the wet ingredients into the dry ingredients.
- Fold in the diced apple.
- Pour the mixture into a greased baking dish and bake for 25-30 minutes, or until golden brown.

Cottage cheese and fresh fruit salad

Ingredients:
- 1/2 cup cottage cheese
- 1 cup mixed fresh fruit (such as berries, kiwi, and pineapple)

Instructions:

- In a bowl, mix together the cottage cheese and mixed fresh fruit.
- Enjoy as a healthy and protein-packed breakfast.

Almond butter and banana on whole grain toast

Ingredients:
- 1 slice whole grain bread
- 1 tbsp almond butter
- 1/2 banana, sliced

Instructions:

- Toast the bread and spread the almond butter on top.
- Add the sliced banana on top of the almond butter.

Green smoothie with kale and pineapple

Ingredients:

- 1 cup kale
- 1/2 cup frozen pineapple
- 1/2 banana
- 1/2 cup unsweetened almond milk
- 1 tbsp honey

Instructions:

- In a blender, mix together the kale, frozen pineapple, banana, almond milk, and honey until smooth.
- Enjoy as a refreshing and nutritious breakfast.

Mushroom and spinach frittata

Ingredients:
- 6 eggs
- 1/2 cup sliced mushrooms
- 1 cup fresh spinach
- 1/4 cup shredded mozzarella cheese
- Salt and pepper to taste
- 1 tbsp olive oil

Instructions:
- Preheat the oven to 350°F.
- In a bowl, beat the eggs with salt and pepper.
- In an oven-safe skillet, sauté the mushrooms and spinach in olive oil over medium heat until tender.
- Pour the eggs over the vegetables and sprinkle with shredded mozzarella cheese.
- Bake for 15-20 minutes, or until set.

Chia pudding with berries

Ingredients:
- 1/4 cup chia seeds
- 1 cup unsweetened almond milk
- 1 tbsp honey
- 1/2 cup mixed berries

Instructions:

- In a bowl, mix together the chia seeds, almond milk, and honey.
- Refrigerate for at least 30 minutes, or until the mixture thickens into a pudding-like consistency.
- Top with mixed berries and enjoy.

Banana and almond butter smoothie

Ingredients:
- 1/2 banana
- 1 tbsp almond butter
- 1/2 cup unsweetened almond milk
- 1 tbsp honey
- 1/4 tsp vanilla extract

Instructions:

- In a blender, mix together the banana, almond butter, almond milk, honey, and vanilla extract until smooth.
- Enjoy as a filling and protein-packed breakfast.

Sweet potato and black bean breakfast bowl

Ingredients:

- 1 medium sweet potato, diced
- 1/2 cup canned black beans, rinsed and drained
- 1/4 avocado, diced
- 1 egg, fried or scrambled
- Salt and pepper to taste
- 1 tbsp olive oil

Instructions:

- In a pan, sauté the diced sweet potato in olive oil over medium heat until tender and lightly browned.
- Add the black beans and cook until heated through.
- Fry or scramble the egg in a separate pan.
- Serve the sweet potato and black bean mixture topped with the fried or scrambled egg and diced avocado.
- Season with salt and pepper to taste.

Quinoa breakfast bowl with fruit and nuts

Ingredients:
- 1/2 cup cooked quinoa
- 1/4 cup plain Greek yogurt
- 1/4 cup mixed fresh fruit (such as berries and mango)
- 1 tbsp chopped nuts (such as almonds or walnuts)
- 1 tbsp honey

Instructions:

- In a bowl, mix together

Quinoa breakfast bowl with fruit and nuts

Ingredients:
- 1/2 cup cooked quinoa
- 1/4 cup plain Greek yogurt
- 1/4 cup mixed fresh fruit (such as berries and mango)
- 1 tbsp chopped nuts (such as almonds or walnuts)
- 1 tbsp honey

Instructions:

- In a bowl, mix together the cooked quinoa and plain Greek yogurt.
- Top with mixed fresh fruit and chopped nuts.
- Drizzle with honey and enjoy as a protein-packed breakfast.

Egg and vegetable muffins

Ingredients:
- 6 eggs
- 1/4 cup diced vegetables (such as bell peppers and onions)
- Salt and pepper to taste
- 1 tbsp olive oil

Instructions:

- Preheat the oven to 350°F.
- In a bowl, beat the eggs with salt and pepper.
- In a non-stick muffin tin, sauté the diced vegetables in olive oil over medium heat until tender.
- Pour the beaten eggs over the vegetables in the muffin tin.
- Bake for 20-25 minutes, or until set.
- Serve warm or refrigerate and enjoy later as a protein-packed breakfast on-the-go.

Berry and yogurt smoothie

Ingredients:
- 1/2 cup mixed frozen berries
- 1/2 cup plain Greek yogurt
- 1/2 cup unsweetened almond milk
- 1 tbsp honey

Instructions:

- In a blender, mix together the mixed frozen berries, plain Greek yogurt, almond milk, and honey until smooth.
- Enjoy as a refreshing and healthy breakfast.

Avocado and egg breakfast sandwich

Ingredients:
- 1 whole grain English muffin, toasted
- 1/4 avocado, mashed
- 1 egg, fried or scrambled
- Salt and pepper to taste

Instructions:

- Toast the whole grain English muffin.
- Spread the mashed avocado on one half of the muffin.
- Fry or scramble the egg in a non-stick pan.
- Place the egg on top of the mashed avocado and season with salt and pepper.
- Top with the other half of the muffin and enjoy.

Spinach and mushroom breakfast wrap

Ingredients:
- 1 whole grain tortilla
- 1/2 cup fresh spinach
- 1/4 cup sliced mushrooms
- 1 egg, fried or scrambled
- 1 tbsp shredded cheddar cheese
- Salt and pepper to taste

Instructions:
- In a non-stick pan, sauté the fresh spinach and sliced mushrooms until tender.
- Fry or scramble the egg in the same pan and season with salt and pepper.
- Place the whole grain tortilla on a plate.
- Top with the sautéed spinach and mushrooms, followed by the fried or scrambled egg.
- Sprinkle shredded cheddar cheese on top and fold the tortilla into a wrap.
- Serve warm and enjoy.

SNACK RECIPES

Baked Sweet Potato Chips

Ingredients:

- 1 large sweet potato
- 1 tablespoon olive oil
- 1/2 teaspoon salt

Instructions:

1. Preheat the oven to 375°F.
2. Slice the sweet potato into thin rounds, about 1/8 inch thick.
3. Toss the sweet potato rounds in olive oil and salt.
4. Arrange the sweet potato rounds on a baking sheet lined with parchment paper.
5. Bake for 20-25 minutes, or until crispy and golden brown.
6. Serve immediately or store in an airtight container for up to 3 days.

Peanut Butter and Banana Bites

Ingredients:

- 1 banana
- 2 tablespoons peanut butter
- 2 tablespoons granola

Instructions:

1. Peel the banana and cut it into thin slices.
2. Spread a small amount of peanut butter on each slice.
3. Sprinkle granola on top of the peanut butter.
4. Serve immediately or store in an airtight container for up to 2 days.

Roasted Chickpeas

Ingredients:

- 1 can chickpeas, drained and rinsed
- 1 tablespoon olive oil
- 1/2 teaspoon garlic powder
- 1/2 teaspoon cumin
- 1/2 teaspoon paprika
- Salt and pepper to taste

Instructions:

1. Preheat the oven to 400°F.
2. Pat the chickpeas dry with a paper towel.
3. Toss the chickpeas in olive oil, garlic powder, cumin, paprika, salt, and pepper.
4. Spread the chickpeas on a baking sheet lined with parchment paper.
5. Bake for 20-25 minutes, or until crispy.
6. Serve immediately or store in an airtight container for up to 3 days.

Spicy Edamame

Ingredients:

- 1 pound frozen edamame, thawed
- 1 tablespoon olive oil
- 1/2 teaspoon garlic powder
- 1/2 teaspoon cayenne pepper
- Salt to taste

Instructions:

1. Preheat the oven to 400°F.
2. In a small bowl, mix together olive oil, garlic powder, cayenne pepper, and salt.
3. Toss the edamame in the spice mixture.
4. Spread the edamame on a baking sheet lined with parchment paper.
5. Bake for 10-12 minutes, or until heated through.
6. Serve immediately or store in an airtight container for up to 3 days.

Greek Yogurt and Berry Parfait

Ingredients:

- 1 cup plain Greek yogurt
- 1/2 cup mixed berries (such as blueberries, raspberries, and strawberries)
- 1/4 cup granola

Instructions:

1. In a small bowl, mix together the Greek yogurt and berries.
2. Layer the yogurt mixture and granola in a small glass or jar.
3. Serve immediately or store in the refrigerator for up to 2 days.

Ants on a Log (Celery Sticks with Peanut Butter and Raisins)

Ingredients:

- 4 celery sticks
- 2 tablespoons peanut butter
- 2 tablespoons raisins

Instructions:

1. Cut the celery sticks into 3-4 inch pieces.
2. Spread peanut butter in the celery groove.
3. Top with raisins.
4. Serve immediately orstore in an airtight container in the refrigerator for up to 2 days.

Mini Caprese Skewers

Ingredients:

- Cherry tomatoes
- Fresh mozzarella balls
- Fresh basil leaves
- Balsamic vinegar (optional)

Instructions:

1. Thread a cherry tomato, a piece of fresh mozzarella, and a fresh basil leaf onto a small skewer or toothpick.
2. Drizzle with balsamic vinegar, if desired.
3. Serve immediately or store in the refrigerator for up to 2 days.

Cucumber and Hummus Bites

Ingredients:

- 1 cucumber
- 1/4 cup hummus

Instructions:

1. Slice the cucumber into thin rounds.
2. Top each cucumber slice with a small spoonful of hummus.
3. Serve immediately or store in an airtight container in the refrigerator for up to 2 days.

Apple and Almond Butter Sandwiches

Ingredients:

- 1 apple
- 2 tablespoons almond butter
- 1 tablespoon honey

Instructions:

1. Slice the apple into thin rounds.
2. Spread almond butter on one slice of apple and drizzle with honey.
3. Top with another slice of apple to make a sandwich.
4. Serve immediately or store in an airtight container in the refrigerator for up to 2 days.

Quinoa and Veggie Stuffed Mini Peppers

Ingredients:

- 1/2 cup cooked quinoa
- 1/4 cup chopped cherry tomatoes
- 1/4 cup chopped cucumber
- 1/4 cup chopped bell pepper
- 1 tablespoon olive oil
- Salt and pepper to taste
- Mini sweet peppers

Instructions:

1. Preheat the oven to 375°F.
2. Place the zucchini rounds on a baking sheet lined with parchment paper.
3. Spoon tomato sauce onto each zucchini round.
4. Top with shredded mozzarella cheese, salt, pepper, and Italian seasoning.
5. Bake for 10-12 minutes, or until the cheese is melted and bubbly.
6. Serve immediately or store in an airtight container in the refrigerator for up to 2 days.

Egg Salad Lettuce Wraps

Ingredients:

- 4 hard-boiled eggs, peeled and chopped
- 2 tablespoons Greek yogurt
- 1 tablespoon Dijon mustard
- 1 tablespoon chopped chives
- Salt and pepper to taste
- 4 large lettuce leaves

Instructions:

1. In a small bowl, mix together the chopped eggs, Greek yogurt, Dijon mustard, chives, salt, and pepper.
2. Spoon the egg salad onto the lettuce leaves.
3. Wrap the lettuce leaves around the egg salad.
4. Serve immediately or store in an airtight container in the refrigerator for up to 2 days.

Zucchini Pizza Bites

Ingredients:

- 2 medium zucchinis
- 1 cup of pizza sauce
- 1 cup of shredded mozzarella cheese
- 1/4 cup of sliced pepperoni
- 1/4 cup of sliced black olives
- 1 teaspoon of dried oregano
- Salt and pepper to taste

Instructions:

1. Preheat your oven to 425°F (218°C).
2. Slice the zucchinis into 1/4-inch thick rounds.
3. Place the zucchini rounds on a baking sheet lined with parchment paper.
4. Season the zucchini rounds with salt and pepper.
5. Spoon a small amount of pizza sauce onto each zucchini round.
6. Top each zucchini round with shredded mozzarella cheese.
7. Add sliced pepperoni and black olives on top of the cheese.
8. Sprinkle dried oregano on top of each zucchini pizza bite.
9. Bake the zucchini pizza bites in the preheated oven for 12-15 minutes, or until the cheese is melted and bubbly.
10. Serve hot and enjoy!

Chocolate Covered Strawberries

Ingredients:

- 1 pint fresh strawberries
- 1/2 cup dark chocolate chips

Instructions:

1. Wash and dry the strawberries.
2. Melt the dark chocolate chips in a microwave-safe bowl, stirring every 15 seconds until melted.
3. Dip each strawberry in the melted chocolate.
4. Place the chocolate-covered strawberries on a baking sheet lined with parchment paper.
5. Refrigerate for 15-20 minutes, or until the chocolate is set.
6. Serve immediately or store in an airtight container in the refrigerator for up to 2 days.

Trail Mix (Nuts, Seeds, and Dried Fruit)

Ingredients:

- 1 cup mixed nuts (such as almonds, cashews, and peanuts)
- 1/2 cup mixed seeds (such as pumpkin and sunflower seeds)
- 1/2 cup dried fruit (such as raisins and cranberries)

Instructions:

1. In a large bowl, mix together the nuts, seeds, and dried fruit.
2. Portion the trail mix into individual snack bags.
3. Serve immediately or store in an airtight container for up to 2 weeks.

Baked Kale Chips

Ingredients:

- 1 bunch kale
- 1 tablespoon olive oil
- Salt and pepper to taste

Instructions:

1. Preheat the oven to 350°F.
2. Wash the kale and remove the leaves from the stems.
3. Pat the kale leaves dry with a paper towel.
4. Toss the kale leaves in olive oil, salt, and pepper.
5. Spread the kale leaves on a baking sheet lined with parchment paper.
6. Bake for 10-12 minutes, or until crispy.
7. Serve immediately or store in an airtight container for up to 3 days.

Cottage Cheese and Pineapple Skewers

Ingredients:

- Cottage cheese
- Fresh pineapple chunks
- Skewers or toothpicks

Instructions:

1. Thread a piece of pineapple and a spoonful of cottage cheese onto a skewer or toothpick.
2. Repeat with remaining pineapple and cottage cheese until all skewers or toothpicks are used. 3. Serve immediately or store in the refrigerator for up to 2 days.

Grilled Shrimp Skewers

Ingredients:

- 1 pound raw shrimp, peeled and deveined
- 1/4 cup olive oil
- 2 tablespoons lemon juice
- 1/2 teaspoon garlic powder
- Salt and pepper to taste
- Skewers

Instructions:

1. Preheat the grill to medium-high heat.
2. In a small bowl, mix together the olive oil, lemon juice, garlic powder, salt, and pepper.
3. Thread the shrimp onto skewers.
4. Brush the shrimp skewers with the olive oil mixture.
5. Grill the shrimp skewers for 2-3 minutes on each side, or until cooked through.
6. Serve immediately or store in an airtight container in the refrigerator for up to 2 days.

Almond Flour Crackers with Guacamole

Ingredients:

- 1 cup almond flour
- 1/4 teaspoon salt
- 1/4 teaspoon garlic powder
- 1 egg
- Guacamole (store-bought or homemade)

Instructions:

1. Preheat the oven to 350°F.
2. In a medium bowl, mix together the almond flour, salt, and garlic powder.
3. Beat the egg in a small bowl.
4. Add the beaten egg to the almond flour mixture and mix until a dough forms.
5. Roll out the dough between two pieces of parchment paper to 1/8 inch thickness.
6. Cut the dough into small squares or rectangles.
7. Place the crackers on a baking sheet lined with parchment paper.
8. Bake for 12-15 minutes, or until lightly golden brown.
9. Serve the almond flour crackers with guacamole.
10. Serve immediately or store in an airtight container for up to 3 days.

Tuna Salad Cucumber Boats

Ingredients:

- 1 can tuna, drained
- 2 tablespoons Greek yogurt
- 1 tablespoon Dijon mustard
- 1 tablespoon chopped chives
- Salt and pepper to taste
- 2 cucumbers

Instructions:

1. In a small bowl, mix together the drained tuna, Greek yogurt, Dijon mustard, chives, salt, and pepper.
2. Cut the cucumbers in half lengthwise and scoop out the seeds to create a hollow center.
3. Fill the cucumber halves with the tuna salad.
4. Serve immediately or store in an airtight container in the refrigerator for up to 2 days.

Roasted Red Pepper and Feta Dip with Veggie Sticks

Ingredients:

- 1 roasted red pepper (store-bought or homemade)
- 4 ounces crumbled feta cheese
- 2 tablespoons Greek yogurt
- 1 tablespoon lemon juice
- Salt and pepper to taste
- Assorted veggie sticks (such as carrots, celery, and bell pepper)

Instructions:

1. In a blender or food processor, blend the roasted red pepper, feta cheese, Greek yogurt, lemon juice, salt, and pepper until smooth.
2. Serve the dip with assorted veggie sticks.
3. Serve immediately or store in an airtight container in the refrigerator for up to 2 days.

DINNER RECIPES

Baked Salmon with Roasted Vegetables

Ingredients:

- 4 salmon fillets
- 2 cups mixed vegetables (such as bell peppers, zucchini, and red onion)
- 2 tbsp olive oil
- Salt and pepper, to taste

Instructions: Preheat the oven to 400°F (200°C). Place the salmon fillets in a baking dish and season with salt and pepper. Toss the mixed vegetables with olive oil, salt, and pepper, and spread them around the salmon in the baking dish. Bake for 15-20 minutes, or until the salmon is cooked through and the vegetables are tender.

Grilled Chicken with Sweet Potato Mash

Ingredients:

- 4 chicken breasts
- 2 sweet potatoes, peeled and cubed
- 2 tbsp olive oil
- Salt and pepper, to taste

Instructions: Preheat the grill to medium-high heat. Season the chicken breasts with salt and pepper, and grill for 6-8 minutes per side, or until cooked through. Meanwhile, boil the sweet potatoes in a pot of salted water until tender. Drain the potatoes and mash them with olive oil, salt, and pepper. Serve the grilled chicken with a side of sweet potato mash.

Beef and Broccoli Stir Fry

Ingredients:

- 1 lb flank steak, sliced into thin strips
- 3 cups broccoli florets
- 1 red bell pepper, sliced
- 1 yellow onion, sliced
- 2 cloves garlic, minced
- 2 tbsp soy sauce
- 1 tbsp honey
- 1 tbsp cornstarch
- 2 tbsp olive oil

Instructions: In a small bowl, whisk together the soy sauce, honey, and cornstarch. Set aside. Heat the olive oil in a large skillet over medium-high heat. Add the sliced flank steak and cook for 2-3 minutes, or until browned. Add the broccoli, bell pepper, onion, and garlic to the skillet, and cook for an additional 3-4 minutes. Pour the soy sauce mixture over the stir fry and cook for another 1-2 minutes, or until the sauce has thickened and the vegetables are tender. Serve hot.

Spicy Shrimp Tacos with Avocado Salsa

Ingredients:

- 1 lb shrimp, peeled and deveined
- 2 tbsp olive oil
- 2 tbsp chili powder
- 1 tsp cumin
- 1/2 tsp garlic powder
- 1/4 tsp cayenne pepper
- Salt and pepper, to taste
- 8 small corn tortillas
- 1 avocado, diced
- 1/4 cup diced red onion
- 1/4 cup chopped fresh cilantro
- Juice of 1 lime

Instructions: In a small bowl, combine the chili powder, cumin, garlic powder, cayenne pepper, salt, and pepper. Toss the shrimp in the spice mixture until coated. Heat the olive oil in a large skillet over medium-high heat. Add the shrimp and cook for 2-3 minutes per side, or until pink and cooked through. In a separate bowl, combine the diced avocado, red onion, cilantro, lime juice, and a pinch of salt. Warm the corn tortillas in

5.

Veggie and Quinoa Stuffed Peppers

Ingredients:

- 4 bell peppers, halved and seeded
- 1 cup cooked quinoa
- 1 cup chopped vegetables (such as zucchini, mushrooms, and carrots)
- 1/2 cup diced onion
- 2 cloves garlic, minced
- 1 tsp dried oregano
- 1 tsp dried basil
- 1/2 tsp salt
- 1/4 tsp black pepper
- 1/4 cup grated Parmesan cheese
- 1 tbsp olive oil

Instructions: Preheat the oven to 375°F (190°C). In a large skillet, heat the olive oil over medium-high heat. Add the chopped vegetables, onion, garlic, oregano, basil, salt, and pepper, and cook until the vegetables are tender. Add the cooked quinoa to the skillet and stir to combine. Fill each bell pepper half with the quinoa and vegetable mixture. Sprinkle the grated Parmesan cheese over the top of the peppers. Place the stuffed peppers in a baking dish and bake for 20-25 minutes, or until the peppers are tender and the cheese is melted and golden brown.

Turkey Meatballs with Zucchini Noodles

Ingredients:

- 1 lb ground turkey
- 1/2 cup breadcrumbs
- 1/4 cup grated Parmesan cheese
- 1 egg
- 2 cloves garlic, minced
- 1 tsp dried oregano
- Salt and pepper, to taste
- 2 zucchini, spiralized
- 1 tbsp olive oil
- 1 cup marinara sauce

Instructions: Preheat the oven to 375°F (190°C). In a large bowl, combine the ground turkey, breadcrumbs, Parmesan cheese, egg, garlic, oregano, salt, and pepper. Mix well and form into meatballs. Place the meatballs on a baking sheet and bake for 20-25 minutes, or until cooked through. In a separate pan, heat the olive oil over medium-high heat. Add the spiralized zucchini and cook for 2-3 minutes, or until tender. Serve the turkey meatballs over the zucchini noodles and top with marinara sauce.

Lemon Garlic Chicken with Asparagus

Ingredients:

- 4 chicken breasts
- 1 lb asparagus, trimmed
- 2 tbsp olive oil
- 2 cloves garlic, minced
- Zest of 1 lemon
- Juice of 1 lemon
- Salt and pepper, to taste

Instructions: Preheat the oven to 400°F (200°C). Place the chicken breasts in a baking dish and season with salt and pepper. Arrange the asparagus around the chicken. In a small bowl, whisk together the olive oil, garlic, lemon zest, and lemon juice. Pour the mixture over the chicken and asparagus. Bake for 20-25 minutes, or until the chicken is cooked through and the asparagus is tender.

Cilantro Lime Shrimp with Cauliflower Rice

Ingredients:

- 1 lb shrimp, peeled and deveined
- 2 tbsp olive oil
- 2 cloves garlic, minced
- Juice of 2 limes
- 1/4 cup chopped cil

- Salt and pepper, to taste
- 1 head cauliflower, grated or riced
- 1 tbsp butter

Instructions: In a large skillet, heat the olive oil over medium-high heat. Add the shrimp and garlic, and cook for 2-3 minutes per side, or until pink and cooked through. Add the lime juice and chopped cilantro to the skillet, and season with salt and pepper. In a separate skillet, melt the butter over medium heat. Add the cauliflower rice and cook for 3-4 minutes, or until tender. Serve the cilantro lime shrimp over the cauliflower rice.

Pork Tenderloin with Apple Cranberry Chutney

Ingredients:

- 1 pork tenderloin
- 1 tbsp olive oil
- Salt and pepper, to taste
- 1 apple, peeled and diced
- 1/4 cup dried cranberries
- 1/4 cup diced red onion
- 1/4 cup apple cider vinegar
- 2 tbsp honey

Instructions: Preheat the oven to 375°F (190°C). Rub the pork tenderloin with olive oil, salt, and pepper. Place the pork in a baking dish and bake for 20-25 minutes, or until cooked through. Meanwhile, in a small saucepan, combine the diced apple, dried cranberries, red onion, apple cider vinegar, honey, and a pinch of salt. Cook over medium heat until the mixture has thickened and the apples are tender. Slice the pork tenderloin and serve with a spoonful of the apple cranberry chutney.

Mushroom and Spinach Risotto

Ingredients:

- 1 cup Arborio rice
- 1 onion, diced
- 2 cloves garlic, minced
- 4 cups vegetable broth
- 1/2 cup white wine
- 1 cup sliced mushrooms
- 2 cups fresh spinach
- 1/4 cup grated Parmesan cheese
- 2 tbsp butter
- Salt and pepper, to taste

Instructions: In a large pot, heat the vegetable broth over medium heat. In a separate pan, sauté the onion and garlic in butter until tender. Add the Arborio rice to the pan and stir to coat with the butter. Add the white wine and cook until the liquid is absorbed. Begin adding the vegetable broth to the rice, 1 cup at a time, stirring constantly and waiting until each cup is absorbed before adding the next. Once all the broth has been added, stir in the sliced mushrooms and spinach. Cook until the mushrooms are tender and the spinach is wilted. Stir in the grated Parmesan cheese and season with salt and pepper.

BBQ Chicken with Roasted Brussel Sprouts

Ingredients:

- 4 chicken breasts
- 1/2 cup BBQ sauce
- 1 lb Brussel sprouts, trimmed and halved
- 2 tbsp olive oil
- Salt and pepper, to taste

Instructions: Preheat the oven to 400°F (200°C). Place the chicken breasts in a baking dish and brush with BBQ sauce. Bake for 20-25 minutes, or until cooked through. In a separate baking dish, toss the halved Brussel sprouts with olive oil, salt, and pepper. Roast the Brussel sprouts in the oven for 15-20 minutes, or until tender and golden brown. Serve the BBQ chicken with a side of roasted Brussel sprouts.

Stuffed Butternut Squash with Quinoa and Kale

Ingredients:

- 2 butternut squash, halved and seeded
- 1 cup cooked quinoa
- 2 cups chopped kale
- 1/2 cup chopped walnuts
- 1/4 cup dried cranberries
- 1/4 cup grated Parmesan cheese
- 2 tbsp olive oil
- Salt and pepper, to taste

Instructions: Preheat the oven to 375°F (190°C). Place the halved butternut squash on a baking sheet and brush with olive oil. Season with salt and pepper. Bake for 35-40 minutes, or until tender. In a separate pan, sauté the chopped kale in olive oil until wilted. Combine the cooked quinoa, sautéed kale, chopped walnuts, dried cranberries, and grated Parmesan cheese in a bowl. Scoop the quinoa mixture into each half of the roasted butternut squash. Bake for an additional 10-15 minutes, or until heated through.

Tuna Salad Lettuce Wraps

Ingredients:

- 2 cans tuna, drained
- 1/4 cup diced red onion
- 1/4 cup diced celery
- 1/4 cup plain Greek yogurt
- 1 tbsp Dijon mustard
- Juice of 1 lemon
- Salt and pepper, to taste
- 8 large lettuce leaves

Instructions: In a bowl, combine the drained tuna, red onion, celery, Greek yogurt, Dijon mustard, lemon juice, salt, and pepper. Mix well. Lay out the lettuce leaves and spoon the tuna salad into the center of each leaf. Wrap the lettuce around the tuna salad, like a burrito. Serve cold.

Grilled Steak with Chimichurri Sauce

Ingredients:

- 2 steaks (such as ribeye or sirloin)
- 1 cup fresh parsley, chopped
- 1/4 cup fresh cilantro, chopped
- 2 cloves garlic, minced
- 1/4 cup red wine vinegar
- 1/4 cup olive oil
- Salt and pepper, to taste

Instructions: Preheat the grill to medium-high heat. Season the steaks with salt and pepper, and grill for 4-5 minutes per side, or until cooked to your liking. In a blender or food processor, combine the chopped parsley, cilantro, minced garlic, red wine vinegar, olive oil, salt, and pepper. Blend until the mixture is smooth. Serve the grilled steaks with a spoonful of chimichurri sauce.

Sweet Potato and Black Bean Chili

Ingredients:

- 1 tbsp olive oil
- 1 onion, diced
- 2 cloves garlic, minced
- 1 red bell pepper, diced
- 1 green bell pepper, diced
- 2 sweet potatoes, peeled and diced
- 2 cans black beans, drained and rinsed
- 1 can diced tomatoes
- 1 cup vegetable broth
- 2 tbsp chili powder
- 1 tbsp cumin
- Salt and pepper, to taste

Instructions: In a large pot, heat the olive oil over medium-high heat. Add the diced onion and garlic, and sauté until tender. Add the diced bell peppers, diced sweet potatoes, black beans, diced tomatoes, vegetable broth, chili powder, cumin, salt, and pepper. Stir to combine. Bring the mixture to a boil, then reduce the heat and simmer for 25-30 minutes, or until the sweet potatoes are tender.

Sesame Ginger Salmon with Broccoli

Ingredients:

- 4 salmon fillets
- 1 tbsp olive oil
- 2 tbsp soy sauce
- 1 tbsp honey
- 2 cloves garlic, minced
- 1 tbsp grated ginger
- 1 tbsp sesame oil
- 1 lb broccoli florets
- Salt and pepper, to taste

Instructions: Preheat the oven to 375°F (190°C). In a small bowl, whisk together the olive oil, soy sauce, honey, minced garlic, grated ginger, and sesame oil. Place the salmon fillets in a baking dish and brush the soy sauce mixture over the top of each fillet. Bake for 12-15 minutes, or until the salmon is cooked through. Meanwhile, steam the broccoli florets until tender. Serve the sesame ginger salmon with a side of steamed broccoli.

Eggplant Rollatini

Ingredients:

- 2 large eggplants, sliced lengthwise
- 2 cups ricotta cheese
- 1 cup grated Parmesan cheese
- 1 egg
- 1 tbsp chopped fresh basil
- 1 tbsp chopped fresh parsley
- 2 cups marinara sauce

Instructions: Preheat the oven to 375°F (190°C). Lay out the eggplant slices and sprinkle with salt. Let sit for 30 minutes, then rinse the eggplant and pat dry with paper towels. In a bowl, mix together the ricotta cheese, grated Parmesan cheese, egg, chopped basil, and chopped parsley. Lay out each eggplant slice and spoon a few tablespoons of the cheese mixture onto each slice. Roll up the eggplant slices and place them seam-side down in a baking dish. Pour the marinara sauce over the top of the eggplant rolls. Bake for 30-35 minutes, or until the eggplant is tender and the sauce is bubbly.

Spicy Sausage and Kale Soup

Ingredients:

- 1 tbsp olive oil
- 1 lb spicy Italian sausage, casings removed
- 1 onion, diced
- 2 cloves garlic, minced
- 4 cups chicken broth
- 2 cups chopped kale
- 1 can diced tomatoes
- 1 can white beans, drained and rinsed
- Salt and pepper, to taste

Instructions: In a large pot, heat the olive oil over medium-high heat. Add the spicy Italian sausage and cook until browned, breaking it up with a spatula. Add the diced onion and minced garlic to the pot and sauté until tender. Add the chicken broth, chopped kale, diced tomatoes, and white beans to the pot. Bring the mixture to a boil, then reduce the heat and simmer for 25-30 minutes, or until the kale is tender and the flavors have melded together. Season with salt and pepper to taste.

Baked Cod with Lemon and Herbs

Ingredients:
- 4 cod fillets
- 2 tbsp olive oil
- 1 tbsp chopped fresh thyme
- 1 tbsp chopped fresh rosemary
- Zest of 1 lemon
- Juice of 1 lemon
- Salt and pepper, to taste

Instructions: Preheat the oven to 375°F (190°C). In a small bowl, mix together the olive oil, chopped fresh thyme, chopped fresh rosemary, lemon zest, and lemon juice. Place the cod fillets in a baking dish and brush the herb mixture over the top of each fillet. Season with salt and pepper. Bake for 15-20 minutes, or until the cod is cooked through and flakes easily with a fork.

Cauliflower Crust Pizza with Pesto and Vegetables

Ingredients:

- 1 head cauliflower, grated
- 1 egg
- 1/2 cup grated Parmesan cheese
- Salt and pepper, to taste
- 1/4 cup pesto
- 1 red bell pepper, sliced
- 1 zucchini, sliced
- 1/2 red onion, sliced
- 1/2 cup shredded mozzarella cheese

Instructions: Preheat the oven to 400°F (200°C). In a large bowl, mix together the grated cauliflower, egg, grated Parmesan cheese, salt, and pepper. Press the cauliflower mixture onto a baking sheet lined with parchment paper, forming a thin crust. Bake the crust for 15-20 minutes, or until golden brown. Spread the pesto over the crust, then top with sliced red bell pepper, sliced zucchini, sliced red onion, and shredded mozzarella cheese. Bake for an additional 10-15 minutes, or until the cheese is melted and bubbly. Slice and serve hot.

DESSERT RECIPES

Chia Seed Pudding

- Ingredients:

    - 1/4 cup chia seeds
    - 1 cup unsweetened almond milk
    - 1 tsp vanilla extract
    - 1 tbsp honey
    -

- Instructions:

    - In a bowl, whisk together chia seeds, almond milk, vanilla extract, and honey until well combined.
    - Cover the bowl and refrigerate for at least 2 hours or overnight.
    - Serve chilled with fresh fruit, nuts, or granola as desired.

Mixed Berry Smoothie Bowl

- Ingredients:

    - 1 cup mixed frozen berries
    - 1 banana
    - 1/2 cup plain Greek yogurt
    - 1/4 cup almond milk
    - 1 tsp honey
- Instructions:
    - In a blender, combine the mixed berries, banana, Greek yogurt, almond milk, and honey.
    - Blend until smooth and creamy.
    - Pour the smoothie into a bowl and top with your favorite toppings such as granola, fresh fruit, and nuts.

Banana Oat Cookies

- Ingredients:
    - 2 ripe bananas, mashed
    - 1 cup rolled oats
    - 1/4 cup peanut butter
    - 1 tsp vanilla extract
- Instructions:
    - Preheat the oven to 350°F (175°C).
    - In a bowl, combine the mashed bananas, rolled oats, peanut butter, and vanilla extract.
    - Mix until well combined.
    - Using a cookie scoop, drop the mixture onto a baking sheet lined with parchment paper.
    - Bake for 15-20 minutes, or until golden brown.

Chocolate Avocado Mousse

- Ingredients:
    - 2 ripe avocados
    - 1/2 cup cocoa powder
    - 1/2 cup unsweetened almond milk
    - 1/4 cup honey
    - 1 tsp vanilla extract
- Instructions:
    - In a blender, combine the avocado flesh, cocoa powder, almond milk, honey, and vanilla extract.
    - Blend until smooth and creamy.
    - Divide the mixture into serving cups and chill for at least 1 hour before serving.

Peanut Butter Banana Bites

- Ingredients:
    - 2 ripe bananas, sliced
    - 1/4 cup peanut butter
    - 1/4 cup dark chocolate chips
- Instructions:
    - Lay the banana slices on a baking sheet lined with parchment paper.
    - Spread peanut butter on half of the banana slices and top with the other half of the banana slices to make sandwiches.
    - Melt the dark chocolate chips in a microwave-safe bowl and drizzle over the banana bites.
    - Freeze for at least 1 hour before serving.

Mixed Fruit Salad

- Ingredients:
    - 2 cups mixed fruit (such as strawberries, blueberries, mango, pineapple, and kiwi)
    - 1 tbsp honey
    - 1 tbsp lime juice
- Instructions:
    - Wash and cut the fruit into bite-sized pieces.
    - In a bowl, whisk together the honey and lime juice.
    - Add the fruit to the bowl and toss with the honey-lime dressing.
    - Chill for at least 30 minutes before serving.

Apple Cinnamon Oat Bars

- Ingredients:
    - 2 cups rolled oats
    - 1/2 cup almond flour
    - 1/4 cup coconut oil
    - 1/4 cup honey
    - 1 tsp cinnamon
    - 1/2 tsp salt
    - 2 cups chopped apples

- Instructions:

    - Preheat the oven to 350°F (175°C) and line a baking dish with parchment paper.
    - In a bowl, mix together the rolled oats, almond flour, coconut oil, honey, cinnamon, and salt until well combined.
    - Fold in the chopped apples.
    - Press the mixture into the baking dish and bake for 30-35 minutes, or until golden brown.
    - Let cool before slicing into bars and serving.

Vanilla Bean Greek Yogurt Popsicles

- Ingredients:
    - 2 cups plain Greek yogurt
    - 1/4 cup honey
    - 1 vanilla bean, scraped
- Instructions:
    - In a bowl, whisk together the Greek yogurt, honey, and vanilla bean until smooth.
    - Pour the mixture into popsicle molds and freeze for at least 4 hours or until firm.
    - Remove from the molds and enjoy.

Mixed Berry Cobbler

- Ingredients:
    - 2 cups mixed berries (such as raspberries, blueberries, and blackberries)
    - 1/2 cup almond flour
    - 1/4 cup honey
    - 1/4 cup coconut oil, melted
    - 1 tsp cinnamon
    - 1/2 tsp salt
- Instructions:
    - Preheat the oven to 350°F (175°C) and grease a baking dish.
    - In a bowl, mix together the mixed berries, almond flour, honey, coconut oil, cinnamon, and salt until well combined.
    - Pour the mixture into the baking dish and bake for 30-35 minutes, or until the top is golden brown and the fruit is bubbly.
    - Let cool before serving.

Coconut Mango Popsicles

- Ingredients:
    - 2 cups fresh mango, chopped
    - 1 can full-fat coconut milk
    - 1/4 cup honey
    - 1 tsp vanilla extract
- Instructions:
    - In a blender, combine the chopped mango, coconut milk, honey, and vanilla extract.
    - Blend until smooth and creamy.
    - Pour the mixture into popsicle molds and freeze for at least 4 hours or until firm.
    - Remove from the molds and enjoy.

Blueberry Lemon Cake Bars

- Ingredients:
    - 2 cups almond flour
    - 1/4 cup coconut oil, melted
    - 1/4 cup honey
    - 2 eggs
    - 1 tsp baking powder
    - 1/2 tsp salt
    - 1 cup fresh blueberries
    - Zest of 1 lemon

- Instructions:

    - Preheat the oven to 350°F (175°C) and grease a baking dish.
    - In a bowl, mix together the almond flour, coconut oil, honey, eggs, baking powder, and salt until well combined.
    - Fold in the blueberries and lemon zest.
    - Pour the mixture into the baking dish and bake for 25-30 minutes, or until golden brown and set.
    - Let cool before slicing into bars and serving.

Peach Oatmeal Bars

- Ingredients:
    - 2 cups rolled oats
    - 1/2 cup almond flour
    - 1/4 cup coconut oil, melted
    - 1/4 cup honey
    - 2 peaches, chopped
    - 1 tsp cinnamon
    - 1/2 tsp salt
- Instructions:
    - Preheat the oven to 350°F (175°C) and grease a baking dish.
    - In a bowl, mix together the rolled oats, almond flour, coconut oil, honey, cinnamon, and salt until well combined.
    - Fold in the chopped peaches.
    - Press the mixture into the baking dish and bake for 25-30 minutes, or until golden brown and set.
    - Let cool before slicing into bars and serving.

Chocolate Dipped Strawberries

- Ingredients:
    - 2 cups fresh strawberries
    - 1/2 cup dark chocolate chips
- Instructions:
    - Wash and dry the strawberries.
    - Melt the dark chocolate chips in a microwave-safe bowl.
    - Dip the strawberries into the melted chocolate and place on a parchment-lined baking sheet.
    - Refrigerate for at least 30 minutes or until the chocolate is firm.

Raspberry Chia Jam

- Ingredients:
    - 2 cups fresh raspberries
    - 2 tbsp chia seeds
    - 1 tbsp honey
- Instructions:
    - In a saucepan, cook the raspberries over medium heat until they start to break down and release their juices.
    - Stir in the chia seeds and honey and cook for an additional 5-10 minutes, or until the mixture has thickened.
    - Let cool before serving.

Cinnamon Apple Chips

- Ingredients:

    - 2 apples, thinly sliced
    - 1 tsp cinnamon

- Instructions:

    - Preheat the oven to 200°F (95°C) and line a baking sheet with parchment paper.
    - Arrange the apple slices on the baking sheet and sprinkle with cinnamon.
    - Bake for 2-3 hours, or until the apple chips are crispy and golden brown.

Pumpkin Spice Energy Balls

- Ingredients:

  - 1 cup rolled oats
  - 1/2 cup almond butter
  - 1/4 cup pumpkin puree
  - 1/4 cup honey
  - 1 tsp pumpkin pie spice

- Instructions:

  - In a bowl, mix together the rolled oats, almond butter, pumpkin puree, honey, and pumpkin pie spice until well combined.
  - Roll the mixture into bite-sized balls.
  - Chill for at least 30 minutes before serving.

Strawberry Shortcake

- Ingredients:
    - 2 cups almond flour
    - 1/4 cup coconut oil, melted
    - 1/4 cup honey
    - 2 eggs
    - 1 tsp baking powder
    - 1/2 tsp salt
    - 2 cups fresh strawberries, sliced
    - Whipped cream (optional)
- Instructions:
    - Preheat the oven to 350°F (175°C) and grease a baking dish.
    - In a bowl, mix together the almond flour, coconut oil, honey, eggs, baking powder, and salt until well combined.
    - Pour the mixture into the baking dish and bake for 25-30 minutes, or until golden brown and set.
    - Let cool before slicing and topping with sliced strawberries and whipped cream (if using).

Lemon Blueberry Cheesecake Bars

- Ingredients:
    - 2 cups almond flour
    - 1/4 cup coconut oil, melted
    - 1/4 cup honey
    - 2 eggs
    - 1 tsp baking powder
    - 1/2 tsp salt
    - 8 oz cream cheese, softened
    - 1/4 cup honey
    - 1 egg
    - 1 tsp vanilla extract
    - 1 cup fresh blueberries
    - Zest of 1 lemon
- Instructions:
    - Preheat the oven to 350°F (175°C) and grease a baking dish.
    - In a bowl, mix together the almond flour, coconut oil, honey, eggs, baking powder, and salt until well combined.
    - Press the mixture into the baking dish and bake for 10-12 minutes, or until lightly golden.
    - In a separate bowl, mix together the cream cheese, honey, egg, vanilla extract, and lemon zest until smooth.
    - Fold in the blueberries.
    - Pour the cream cheese mixture over the baked crust and bake for an additional 20-25 minutes, or until set.
    - Let cool before slicing into bars and serving.

Carrot Cake Muffins

- Ingredients:
    - 2 cups almond flour
    - 1 tsp baking powder
    - 1/2 tsp baking soda
    - 1/2 tsp salt
    - 1 tsp cinnamon
    - 1/2 tsp nutmeg
    - 1/4 cup coconut oil, melted
    - 1/4 cup honey
    - 2 eggs
    - 1 cup shredded carrots
    - 1/4 cup chopped walnuts (optional)
- Instructions:
    - Preheat the oven to 350°F (175°C) and line a muffin tin with paper liners.
    - In a bowl, mix together the almond flour, baking powder, baking soda, salt, cinnamon, and nutmeg until well combined.
    - In a separate bowl, mix together the coconut oil, honey, and eggs until well combined.
    - Add the wet ingredients to the dry ingredients and mix until just combined.
    - Fold in the shredded carrots and chopped walnuts (if using).
    - Spoon the batter into the muffin tin, filling each about 3/4 full.
    - Bake for 20-25 minutes, or until lightly golden and a toothpick inserted in the center comes out clean.

Blackberry Coconut Pudding

- Ingredients:
    - 2 cups fresh blackberries
    - 1 can full-fat coconut milk
    - 1/4 cup honey
    - 1 tsp vanilla extract
- Instructions:
    - In a blender, combine the blackberries, coconut milk, honey, and vanilla extract.
    - Blend until smooth and creamy.
    - Pour the mixture into serving cups and chill for at least 1 hour before serving.

Review This Book

Customer reviews

★★★★½ 4.7 out of 5

5,322 global ratings

5 star	▇▇▇▇▇▇▇	77%
4 star	▇▇	18%
3 star	▏	4%
2 star		1%
1 star		1%

⌄ How customer reviews and ratings work

Thank you for reading this far! I would be extremely grateful if you could take 1 minute of your time to leave a review on Amazon about my work.

Made in United States
North Haven, CT
28 April 2023